Praise for
That Crumpled Paper Was Due Last Week

"*That Crumpled Paper Was Due Last Week* provides an innovative and practical approach to helping boys find success. Ana Homayoun presents straightforward, easily implementable solutions that will help transform the lives of boys and parents. A wonderful read!"

—Michael Gurian, author of *The Wonder of Boys* and *The Minds of Boys*

"Ana Homayoun gets it! Combining an extraordinary feel for what boys face in schools these days with an enormously shrewd, practical set of tips on how to get organized and excel, this book hits a home run. All parents and teachers as well as students (yes, I think girls could find it useful, too!) will find that this book makes school less of a struggle and more of a pleasure. Brief, to the point, and clear, this book is an invaluable, unique tool."

—Edward Hallowell, MD, author of
Superparenting for ADD and *Driven to Distraction*

"Filled with practical advice for the parents of disorganized boys (and that's an awful lot of young boys), Ana Homayoun's *That Crumpled Paper Was Due Last Week* teaches us how to help our sons navigate through a school environment that is less than kind to distracted and disorganized young men."

—Madeline Levine, PhD, author of *The Price of Privilege*

That Crumpled Paper Was Due Last Week

Helping Disorganized and Distracted Boys
Succeed in School and Life

ANA HOMAYOUN

A PERIGEE BOOK

A PERIGEE BOOK
Published by the Penguin Group
Penguin Group (USA) Inc.
375 Hudson Street, New York, New York 10014, USA
Penguin Group (Canada), 90 Eglinton Avenue East, Suite 700, Toronto, Ontario M4P 2Y3, Canada
(a division of Pearson Penguin Canada Inc.)
Penguin Books Ltd., 80 Strand, London WC2R 0RL, England
Penguin Group Ireland, 25 St. Stephen's Green, Dublin 2, Ireland (a division of Penguin Books Ltd.)
Penguin Group (Australia), 250 Camberwell Road, Camberwell, Victoria 3124, Australia
(a division of Pearson Australia Group Pty. Ltd.)
Penguin Books India Pvt. Ltd., 11 Community Centre, Panchsheel Park, New Delhi—110 017, India
Penguin Group (NZ), 67 Apollo Drive, Rosedale, North Shore 0632, New Zealand
(a division of Pearson New Zealand Ltd.)
Penguin Books (South Africa) (Pty.) Ltd., 24 Sturdee Avenue, Rosebank, Johannesburg 2196,
South Africa

Penguin Books Ltd., Registered Offices: 80 Strand, London WC2R 0RL, England

While the author has made every effort to provide accurate telephone numbers and Internet addresses at the time of publication, neither the publisher nor the author assumes any responsibility for errors, or for changes that occur after publication. Further, the publisher does not have any control over and does not assume any responsibility for author or third-party websites or their content.

First edition: January 2010

Library of Congress Cataloging-in-Publication Data

Homayoun, Ana.
    That crumpled paper was due last week : helping disorganized and distracted boys succeed in school and life / Ana Homayoun.— 1st ed.
        p.   cm.
    "A Perigee Book."
    Includes bibliographical references and index.
    ISBN 978-0-399-53559-8
    1. Boys—United States—Life skills guides.   2. Parenting—United States.   3. Success—Psychological aspects.   4. Time management.   I. Title.
    HQ775.H75 2010
    649'.132—dc22   2009033220

PRINTED IN THE UNITED STATES OF AMERICA
20   19   18   17   16   15   14   13   12   11

This book describes the real experiences of real people. The author has disguised the identities of some, and in some instances created composite characters, but none of these changes has affected the truthfulness and accuracy of her story. Penguin is committed to publishing works of quality and integrity. In that spirit, we are proud to offer this book to our readers; however, the story, the experiences and the words are the author's alone.

To Mrs. Ellen Goldberg, my fourth grade teacher, who taught me the importance of looking for and respecting the personal potential within myself and in others.

To my parents, Amir and Bahereh, whose own dreams paved the way for my possibilities.

CONTENTS

INTRODUCTION

Many educators and researchers believe there is currently a crisis in boys' education, and if you've picked up this book, you may already be aware of it. Male students are, on average, between six months and a year behind their female counterparts when they start high school, and the girls stay ahead right through their senior year.

The problem is clear to the parents who come into my office for the first time, typically at their wits' end and sometimes near tears. The boy that they know to be smart, witty, thoughtful, and/or brilliant can't remember to turn in his homework and is failing several classes. The son who was absolutely precious as a young child started slipping as a middle schooler and has now become a headache of a teenager who just this morning forgot his English essay on the printer, has no idea that he has two tests tomorrow, and still needs to return his uniform for a school sport that ended two weeks ago.

Sound familiar?

If you're one of these troubled parents, you know that today's academic environment is exponentially more challenging than the one in which you grew up—and in ways that tend to be more difficult for boys than for girls. Research suggests that boys often struggle with certain kinds of multi-tasking, and yet schools often ask them to juggle seven different classes, short- and long-term assignments, and multiple sports and activities, all while they are going through puberty. But even armed with this knowledge and a lot of encouragement, the parents I meet for the first time in my office still can't seem to help their sons get ahead and stay ahead of their workload and schedule. Why? Because they don't have the *tools* to arm their sons for the challenges they face, and too often the result is frustration, fights, and, sadly, a bright boy convinced he can't succeed. Without the essential tools to thrive as students and as individuals, these boys are at risk of giving up before ever finding their own true version of success.

> Without the essential tools to thrive as students and as individuals, these boys are at risk of giving up before ever finding their own true version of success.

So what's a parent to do in the face of this seemingly stacked deck? The answer is surprisingly simple; you help your son take control of his heavy load of responsibilities by using organizational techniques *specifically designed for preteen and teenage boys*. These tools allow him to focus on each task, one at a time, until each one is taken care of, essentially transforming a daunting multi-tasking challenge—dealing with homework, sports, activities, family life, and the social scene—into a more tangible single-tasking effort; that is, doing one thing at a time, and doing it well. Once that hardwired organizational hurdle is overcome, your son's natural enthusiasm, intelligence, and vigor are unleashed and available to propel him toward success in academics and life.

This book describes those techniques in detail, and it's a result of my years of hands-on experience as an educational consultant, working with situations like yours. Most important, it's designed to work for *your* family, in *your* home. Over the years, parents have taken the techniques I offer here and applied them to their own situations with great success, whether their families are well-to-do or of modest means; nuclear or multi-household; large or small. Disorganization crosses all economic and ethnic barriers, and my experience demonstrates that boys as young as the fifth and sixth grade can adapt incremental habits that help them feel more organized, motivated, and in control of their own destiny. Although I can say with complete assurance that these tools aren't magic, the results have been described by more than one parent as "miraculous."

I still remember a spring afternoon when the problem of disorganized and vulnerable boys came into sharp focus for me. I'd founded Green Ivy Educational Consulting a few years before, and through my academic training and our experience in the office working with young people, I'd already developed most of the organizational system and study tips outlined in this book.

However, on this particular day I was meeting with the parents of a tenth grade boy. The young man was getting mostly Cs and was generally disorganized and underprepared. Midway through our meeting, the father looked desperately at me and asked, "Ana, be straight with me—is my son the only one like this?" I hesitated and quickly ran through our client list in my head. I realized at that moment that nearly 75 percent of our students were boys, and I confirmed then what I had suspected all along, that the young men we were working with weren't unusual at all. I grew to understand more and more how boys are often different from girls when it comes to organization, time management, and study skills—a fact well known to many parents with both sons and daughters.

I shouldn't have been surprised—in my work with hundreds of kids I'd discovered that only rarely were the boys' failures due to difficulties with the classroom material. Instead, symptoms of chronic disorganization—losing completed homework, forgetting about tests, and not turning in assignments—were by far the bigger culprits in their dismal performance. And worse, because these failures also diminished their personal self-confidence and self-esteem, these boys had started to see themselves as failures in *all* aspects of their lives—a very sad and scary progression, which led to even more misery and disillusionment.

As I helped some of these students become better organized and more able to effectively and efficiently complete their schoolwork, I watched the same boys who walked into my office with five brown grocery bags' worth of unsorted school papers become young men who planned out their time and turned in their assignments when they were due. But more important, over time I also witnessed an amazing transformation in their personal self-confidence and self-esteem. As they began to improve in school, these boys began to explore, dream, and discover a level of success they had previously thought unfathomable—in essence, they set their mind to achieve what were once their craziest dreams, and over time, those dreams started to come true. One young man received a scholarship to a school that was once academically out of reach, and another snagged a walk-on spot to a Division I basketball program a mere two years after he was warming the bench as a member of his junior varsity basketball team.

> As they began to improve in school, these boys began to explore, dream, and discover a level of success they had previously thought unfathomable—in essence, they set their mind to achieve what were once their craziest dreams, and over time, those dreams started to come true.

And it is not just the amazing, transformative experiences that are worth noting; often what we see emerge is the boy who smiles a little wider, who has a new twinkle in his eye because he believes in himself or delivers witty jokes that he was once too self-conscious to crack.

Those are the changes that, while seemingly minor, are actually quite monumental.

So while the strategies in this book have helped students improve their grades and test scores, the goal of my work is much more than merely increasing numbers. Ultimately, my hope for children has always been that they are able to develop their self-confidence, resiliency, and accountability so that they become active and productive members of their own community and our greater society as a whole.

In the end, though, the strategies I use are effective because they are accessible, sensible, and easy to implement. Though this book was written to address the specific needs and unique challenges of working with preteen and teenage boys, many of these strategies can also be successfully implemented for girls who struggle with organization and time management.

On the pages that follow, you will find a specific process to help you create an environment in which your child can develop and maintain organization and time-management skills. Each chapter focuses on a unique aspect of the method and includes a checklist highlighting the main strategies and ideas of that chapter, making it simple to put the ideas into practice in your home. I explain the strategies alongside real-life success stories of young men I've helped over the years—boys like those I just mentioned, whose transformation has been deemed a "miracle" by their parents, guidance counselors, and teachers. To protect the privacy of the students I've worked with and their families, I have changed their names and other identifying particulars, and I have created composite characters wherever possible.

A final note before you dive in: Results, as with most things, do not typically happen overnight, and consistency is key. Some boys take longer than others, some get off track (I include specific techniques to address such circumstances and get them going again), but I have often found that many boys make the monumental shift six months to a year after the strategies are first introduced to them.

In fact, just this afternoon I checked my email to find a message from a mother with whom I had consulted briefly six months ago:

> *Dear Ana,*
> *HE FINALLY GETS IT!*

I hope, that with the help of these proven strategies your son will soon get it as well.

1

Why Boys Struggle with Organization and Time Management

Let me tell you about a tall, lanky, and bright boy named James.

James and his mother, Miriam, walked into my office for the first time a few years ago. At the time, James was a sophomore in high school who performed extremely well on standardized tests but was getting no better than Cs in his classes. Moreover, he was in danger of spending his entire vacation in summer school. I still remember the defeated looks on both James's and Miriam's faces when I first saw them. James was carrying two backpacks, one slung over each shoulder, and Miriam followed with three brown grocery bags full of school papers she had gathered from here and there around the house.

"I don't know if these are important or not," she told me wearily, "but I'm uncomfortable throwing them out." She shot James an annoyed look, which he returned.

Although James was quite irritated to be working with me—he made it very clear he would rather be spending his Saturdays playing golf—we got started quickly. We located his planner, which he had stopped using long ago, and then began to organize his binders. While we worked I asked him about his life—activities, hobbies, pets—and I got back mostly one-word responses grudgingly peppered with a few actual phrases. After a couple of hours together, we had sorted through every single piece of paper and created seven organized binders. In the process, we also recycled two trees' worth of paper. When we finished, James actually seemed reenergized and relieved. Where there had been crumpled papers and disorder, there was now a simple system in place, and he had a fresh start.

Over the course of his next two years in high school, James became one of the most organized students I worked with—barely a paper out of place, consistently using his planner, and generally staying on top of things. He'd realized along the way that the better organized he was, the more time he could spend hanging out with his friends and playing golf, in other words, the things he *enjoyed* doing. His grades improved, as did his general all-around disposition—in particular a natural, dry wit began to appear more and more as his confidence grew. When he first came into our office, he seemed reserved and sullen, but over time, he became relaxed and quick with a snappy comeback whenever he wasn't too excited about the task at hand.

> He'd realized along the way that the better organized he was, the more time he could spend hanging out with his friends and playing golf, in other words, the things he *enjoyed* doing.

But it wasn't just his success inside the classroom that was crucial for his personal development. In his senior year—after much coaxing and encouragement—James had gotten a summer job at a local manufacturing facility, and the experience helped his personal and professional skills flourish. For one of the first times in his life, he was solely accountable and responsible for himself and his actions. He showed up on time, was efficient, and developed great working relationships with his colleagues, who came from many different backgrounds. He got rave reviews for his work, which helped solidify his notion that he could be a success—on his terms, in his own way.

One recent afternoon, as I was working on this book, one of my associates appeared at my office door and told me a parent was in the waiting room to see me. I walked out to find Miriam, and I couldn't help but flash back to the way she had looked that first visit, her defeated expression.

But this time was different. She was beaming.

"I just stopped by to tell you how well James is doing," she said. "He just loves college." She went on to tell me that he seemed happy, confident, and independent.

"For three years, though," she admitted, "I thought I was banging my head against the wall."

It was true, James's success wasn't immediate, but here was Miriam, bubbling over about the ways James's confidence, work ethic, and personal accountability had flourished over the past year. She just couldn't wait to give me the good news in person.

Although each child has his own gifts, strengths, and struggles, James is typical of the boys I work with. The truth is that preteen and teenage boys think differently, act differently, and often process information differently from their female counterparts, and as a group, they are consequently lagging behind girls in school achievement. It's not just about grades, though—it's the way this lag translates into lower academic self-confidence and self-esteem, issues that worry many educators and sociologists, who tend to agree that this gender gap seems worse now than in the past.

Although each student's individual personality and circumstances play a role, there are five basic factors I see when working with preteen and teenage boys:

- Trouble with multi-tasking
- Over-involved parents

- Technology distractions

- Sleep deprivation

- Fear of making wrong choices

For some boys, all of these factors play a role in their challenges with organization and time management; other boys may struggle with just one or two. It's also important to realize that the factors affecting your son may change over time. A seventh grader who struggles with multi-tasking, for instance, may become a high school sophomore who is distracted by technology and exhausted from sleep deprivation. Let's look at each one in more detail.

Challenge 1: The Reality of Multi-Tasking

First and foremost, we (and by *we*, I mean schools, parents, and educators) ask boys to multi-task in school more than ever before, and yet research shows that this kind of academic juggling is tougher for boys than for girls. Thirty years ago, most sixth graders had one teacher for most of their academic classes—now students often have three or four different academic instructors (and sometimes more), with different expectations and procedures. Some of these preteen and teenage boys find themselves juggling seven classes, extracurricular activities, sports, and a social life, all while going through puberty. These boys struggle to set priorities, in part because every coach and teacher says that they "have to give it their all, *all* the time." For instance, some boys who play baseball don't just practice baseball—they have batting practice, team practice, hitting coaches, and conditioning. Academically, they've got homework, long- and short-term projects, outside reading, makeup work, and research. Just thinking about it is enough to make even a well-organized adult tired.

Scientists have discovered in recent years that the brains of men and women seem to be wired differently; women can more easily handle language-based multi-tasking—writing notes while listening to someone speak, for instance—while men are superior at spatial-based multi-tasking, which comes in handy in sports and videogames, but is rarely any help in the classroom.

Some of these preteen and teenage boys find themselves juggling seven classes, extracurricular activities, sports, and a social life, all while going through puberty.

There is other evidence that boys are more likely to be kinesthetic learners—students who naturally prefer to take in information physically by carrying out a task rather than seeing or hearing about it. They may do well in their school's chemistry laboratory, for instance, while struggling with the same chemical equations that underlie that lab work.

Recent brain research specifically centered on adolescents also finds that regardless of sex, the teenager's prefrontal cortex—that part of the brain that can be likened to the body's CEO because it regulates behavior, organizes thoughts, and assesses risks—is far less developed than the reasoning centers of the brain. In other words, teens are capable of wondrous leaps of intellectual and artistic achievement, but the part of the brain that would help them manage these insights isn't ready yet. Although there is a wide range of normal ages, on average, boys end puberty as many as three years later than girls, which makes for a double whammy—even if they *were* wired the same way as girls to do the mental juggling needed for modern schoolwork, their brains wouldn't be quite ready yet to manage it all, at least not without significant help.

What this means is that as their bodies are continuing to develop, boys are being asked to juggle all of these different aspects of their lives without any clear-cut system or method for organizing and managing their time.

What this means is that as their bodies are continuing to develop, boys are being asked to juggle all of these different aspects of their lives without any clear-cut system or method for organizing and managing their time. Even if they wanted to come up with their own system, most boys lack the ability to create something that works, and they become frustrated with their inability to feel in control and on top of their situation. Parents, in turn, become frustrated and disappointed with their son's inability to find success, which causes even more stress.

We could argue that a seismic change in the educational landscape is necessary, but through my work, I have been able to help boys make *incremental* changes that transform their studying and organizational habits. Because boys struggle with multi-tasking, I realized that developing a system that allows them to focus on *singular tasks*—one at a time—is one of the crucial elements in helping boys find their own personal success.

Challenge 2: The Parent Crutch

Some moms who come into my office are terrifically organized—nearly perfectly so, with color-coded calendars, BlackBerrys, hands-free headsets—and they wonder why their sons are so *dis*organized. Part of the problem is, of course, that with Mom so on top of it, these sons have never been forced to develop such skills on their own. When confronted with the need to organize themselves, they consequently react with frustration and, finally, give up on organization altogether.

This is not to say that involvement in your children's education isn't vital and irreplaceable. Study after study finds that as the level of parental involvement increases, academic performance tends to increase along with it. Parents on the whole are much more involved in their children's schoolwork now than anytime since the advent of the modern educational system as we know it.

But the truth is that some parents are so *overly* involved (sometimes unintentionally) that their children are not given the chance to develop their own skills and motivation. The so-called helicopter parent, a term first coined by the authors Foster Cline and Jim Fay in 1990, can have a stifling effect on a boy who is ready to master self-reliance, self-regulation, and responsibility but who is never given the freedom to try (and even to fail).

Dan was a senior with whom I worked a few years ago. We were finishing up our meeting, and he wanted to schedule another appointment, but as I opened my calendar, he turned to me and said that he would have his mother email me to set it up.

"Why?" I asked.

He hemmed and hawed and finally said it was because he didn't know his own schedule.

"Dan," I said, "you've got a car, you're doing well in school, you've got your binder organized and everything. You're eighteen and can go vote and even go defend your country, but you can't figure out if you can be somewhere at 4:00 p.m. on a Tuesday?"

He smiled sheepishly at me. "I can," he said. "I just never had to."

"Well," I said, "it's nice to have a part-time secretary, but do you really need one?"

From that point on Dan put his appointments in his planner right next to his assignments and other responsibilities and soon thereafter had no trouble scheduling his next appointments.

Often parents worry that if left to their own devices, their sons will just plain get it *wrong*. For example, some parents complete their son's college applications because they think that their sons are too busy or will write the wrong thing or it would just be faster to do something themselves. In actuality, it would be a great teachable moment for their son. Even well-intentioned parents (and I like to think that most parents are well intentioned) can inadvertently discourage their son's ability to develop and maintain his own organizational system.

But how does your son develop these skills, even with an appropriate level of help from you? Simply following your example will probably not lead to a huge improvement in organizational skills—after all, very few preteen or adolescent boys seek to do anything that even remotely resembles what their parents are doing.

> Simply following your example will probably not lead to a huge improvement in organizational skills—after all, very few preteen or adolescent boys seek to do anything that even remotely resembles what their parents are doing.

This book provides a framework for an appropriate level of parental participation, with plenty of examples, checklists, suggestions, and, yes, cautions, so that you can help your son develop his own organizational abilities without either depending too heavily on yours or floundering on his own.

Challenge 3: The Lure of Technology

It's easy to underestimate the effect technology has on our lives. I check my email and listen to my iPod, and I appreciate the extent to which gadgetry has, in some ways, enhanced our lives. However, when it comes to teenage boys, technology can create a challenging distraction that can make it difficult for them to focus or prioritize, even if that technology is ostensibly used to help them study, such as a home computer.

Imagine your easily distractible son using his computer under the guise of doing homework and having it *ding* every time he gets an instant message or email from that girl he likes asking him "Whtz up?" It also plays his favorite music, videos, movies, and now TV shows. How can his less-than-enthralling English assignment compete? The truth is, it can't. The computer, without sensible regulation, is far too distracting.

In its own way, technology creates multiple avenues for multi-tasking—instant messaging while writing a paper, for instance—that get in the way of the single-purpose organizational model boys need. My organizational and time-management system does not discount technology and its many benefits, including the significant advantages of using a computer for research and word processing. I do, however, focus on avoiding distractions while using computers and other aids when appropriate.

Challenge 4: Sleep Deprivation

It's no secret that most kids are really tired. Because they are over-scheduled and need plenty of sleep to accompany their growth spurt, many preteens and teenagers easily find themselves with extreme sleep deficits. In fact, your adolescent son has his biology working against him during these years; changes in his brain cause him to be gearing up for intense thought late at night, just as his circadian clock is trying to wind him down for his needed rest. What happens most often is the growing and changing brain wins the battle, keeping active well past 11:00. School schedules being what they are, your son will then be urged out of bed as early as 7:00 (or possibly earlier if he's involved in certain sports, clubs, or academic supports), and rarely will he get his needed nine and a quarter hours of sleep; he'll be short at least an hour. This often leads to feelings of crankiness, grogginess, and general annoyance about anything and everything. It also can seriously affect his school performance.

While there is a new concern about teens and sleep habits (including campaigns in many communities to push back ever-earlier school starting times), there isn't a lot a boy can do to change schedules that are out of his control. However, something I often hear from kids who use my system to become better organized and manage their time is that they are able to get to bed earlier at night, and for many of them, this prospect is incredibly exciting!

Last year, when Mike came into my office for the first time to get organized, we talked about his habits, goals, and plans. A junior and one of the top baseball players at his high school, he was hoping to be recruited to play in college but needed to get his grades up to at least a 3.0 GPA. His schedule was tough—he spent hours in the gym, and that left precious little time for everything else he had to fit in. Although he seemed a bit agitated and restless, he was also clearly a hardworking kid with a good work ethic, and he quickly saw how adding organization and time management would help him fulfill his goals both in and out of the classroom.

When he came in a few weeks later, he seemed calmer, and I asked how things were going.

"Ana," he said. "I'm getting to bed a full hour and a half sooner every night now." He felt calmer and more focused and seemed less stressed. We quickly did the math, which worked out to nearly eight hours more sleep a week.

> It's important to remember that time management not only gives boys more time for schoolwork and activities but can also be just what they need to get back on track to a healthy level of rest.

It's important to remember that time management not only gives boys more time for schoolwork and activities but can also be just what they need to get back on track to a healthy level of rest.

Challenge 5: The Crippling Fear of the Unwise Choice

On my desk, there is a paperweight with the saying, What would you do if you knew you could not fail? I bought it back when I was just starting my work with students because even though teaching organization to teenagers was a terribly big leap from my former job working in finance, I loved working with students, and knew it was what I was meant to do.

More and more, there is a thinly veiled fear of risk, and especially of failure, among many parents and students. They panic, thinking that whatever they do might not be the *right* thing to do to get into the *right* college and get the *right* job (which would lead to the *right* spouse and the *right* kids—ad infinitum). *Decisions and choices that are probably best determined years later instead become distracting and crippling dilemmas today.* In some cases this fear of the unwise choice actually prevents students from finding their own voices and pursuing their own interests. Well-intentioned parents become over-involved in their children's lives because they become worried that their children won't do something right (like finishing a term paper or applying to college) and their children's whole future will go out the window.

A few years back, I was working with a young man who was applying to college; Steve had worked himself into a real frenzy over what he was going to write for his college essay. He was a talented writer, but this fear of "What is the right thing to say?" or "What are they going to want to hear?" had him paralyzed. Everything he wrote seemed forced and trite, and his personal voice was completely lost. His writings seemed like an exercise in second-guessing the admissions officials rather than an opportunity for him to share his wit, wisdom, and charisma (with which he was truly blessed!).

> Well-intentioned parents become over-involved in their children's lives because they become worried that their children won't do something right (like finishing a term paper or applying to college) and their children's whole future will go out the window.

One day I had a little epiphany and asked him to write a short essay imagining his perfect day—who he would spend it with, what he would do, and where he would go.

"Ana," he said, "I don't get it. Why would a college admissions officer want to hear about my perfect day?"

"Forget that for now," I replied. "Just write this piece as if you had nothing else to do this weekend. Write about you and your own personal dream day."

A few days later, he came in with an essay that was heartfelt, creative, and far better than anything else he had written—because his true voice finally came through. His personal statement now revealed that he was a person with a great group of friends who would spend his school lunches eating a burrito before playing intramural sports (truly a teenage-boy scenario—eating a bean burrito and then running around for thirty minutes!), who loved writing for the sports section of the school paper and hoped that every physics test was permanently postponed, and whose ideal day would end with an hour-long Steven Colbert special.

In essence, Steve revealed what I knew was true—he was a real person with likes and dislikes, dreams and aspirations. After working through a few drafts, Steve submitted that essay with the majority of his college applications. All too often, the underlying fear of choosing correctly can erase what's really important and authentic about a boy and can lead to a lost sense of self. Organization and time-management skills help boys focus on what really motivates them and give them practice and experience achieving the steps toward making it happen, thus restoring their self-confidence and belief in their ability to succeed.

How This Book Can Help

I designed this book based on my work with parents (and this includes anyone raising a boy, such as grandparents, aunts, uncles, etc.) and disorganized boys, and I address each of the challenges that contributes to disorganization in its own part of the book, offering strategies on replacing multi-tasking with compartmentalizing, dialing back parental involvement so that boys go through their own struggles (and ultimately find their own success), and alleviating the ever-present distraction of technology. The strategies in this book are designed for boys who are currently in middle school and high school, though certain elements can certainly be modified for boys in younger grades.

My direct work with students has taught me that the better organized students are, the faster they tend to get their assignments done and the more time they have to pursue their own personal goals—whether those goals be academic, athletic, extracurricular, or otherwise. In doing so, boys are able to work on developing their sense of self, so they have more confidence in their personal abilities. This book is just as much about helping boys develop goals and personal character as it is about creating organized binders and to-do lists and studying properly for the next algebra test.

> This book is just as much about helping boys develop goals and personal character as it is about creating organized binders and to-do lists and studying properly for the next algebra test.

Remember, while your son may feel defeated and fear failure, chances are he's never been given the right tools to make a difference. You'll find those tools throughout the next chapters. These strategies work, and together we'll figure out how to make them work for *your* family.

Summary

No child exists in a vacuum, and if your son is struggling with organization and time-management challenges, he's likely dealing with lots of issues at once:

- There's evidence that boys may be less adept at the kind of multi-tasking required in today's schools.

- Today's parents can often inadvertently micromanage their children's lives, preventing their sons from independently developing the very organizational skills they require to be successful.

- Technological distractions are everywhere (including in boys' study spaces), with their seductive siren songs of social networking and fantasy role-playing.

- Ironically, many boys who do manage to juggle all the responsibilities and temptations surrounding them end up paying a heavy price for that "success" in lost sleep and find themselves with the additional burden of the health issues arising from that deficit.

- Today's kids are presented with so many choices at such an early age, the pressure to choose among them—and choose wisely—is greater than ever.

2

Approach and Attitude

How Parents Factor into the Equation

When distressed parents call my office for the first time, I can usually hear the tension through the phone line. Their son, who is so bright and talented in many respects, is not doing well at school, and his disorganization and poor academic performance are obviously causing an underlying stress to family systems and dynamics. I can sense the tears of frustration, the yelling, the general disgust and feelings of failure—and that's just the parents!

It's a cycle of negativity that becomes damaging, because these anxieties are transferred back to the student. Think about it: you return from a parent–teacher conference feeling helpless, your spouse then gets angry, and you both feel overwhelmed. Meanwhile all the lost homework, missing assignments, sloppiness, and general disarray have your son feeling tense already, and when your frustration gets added to the picture, the combination makes him start to feel even worse about himself. For many of these boys, it's just easier to give up and feel like a failure than to try, because they have always felt as if they *are* doing their best—it's just that they have not found the right tools or the right system to help them succeed with long-term results. This kind of negativity can easily loom large over a household; hundreds of parents I have talked to over the years know that the stress of disorganization and poor academic performance can derail an entire household.

When I met Diane and her family, dinners at their house were, in two words, *not fun*. Diane is an MBA-educated former corporate businesswoman with two teenagers, fifteen-year-old Scott and seventeen-year-old Lisa. Her affable husband is a successful businessman, and Diane decided to stay home and spend more time with their children. Scott was a freshman in high school, a quiet and unassuming young man who forgot about half of his stuff on the kitchen counter on his way out the door to school. Almost every morning, it seemed, Diane lunged after Scott to give him his lunch, his math book, and the English essay that he left on the printer. She had to drop so many things off at school that she was on a first-name basis with the front-office clerk at his high school—and the high school is a fairly large one, with over sixteen hundred students.

Diane wanted Scott to do well and was worried that every missing homework assignment or poor test grade would jeopardize his chances of getting into a "good" college, especially because more students than ever are applying to college. Frustrated from spending half of her mornings as Scott's secretary, she tended to lash out at him with common refrains of, "You always forget things!" and "When are you going to be more responsible?" Scott, in response, retreated further, feeling a combination of deep-seated guilt because he was doing so poorly in school and hesitation because he was afraid that anything he said could potentially set off his mom.

Diane really and truly loved her son and was a wonderful mother, but she had let herself become too emotionally invested in Scott's disorganization. The rest of the family (even the dogs!) kept their heads down, hoping to avoid the whole situation and refrain from creating any additional tension. Part of the problem was Diane's approach—she took his disorganization and lack of study skills as a reflection of *her* success (or failure) as a parent. Because she took it so personally, her approach was not getting either one of them results and had just led to increased tension in the household.

In my experience, positive parental approaches and attitudes are key elements to helping children become better organized, independent, and self-reliant young people. I meet a lot of parents who feel personally embarrassed and guilty about their son's poor academic performance, detachment from school, and general malaise. Yet by complaining about their son's shortcomings, they are actually (unwittingly) creating a more toxic environment. The parents who come into my office assuming the worst of their child ("He never gets it . . . he's always doing this") are often the ones digging their children—and themselves—a bigger hole, complete with the emotional baggage that makes it more difficult for their children to become organized, responsible, and accountable.

> The parents who come into my office assuming the worst of their child ("He never gets it . . . he's always doing this") are often the ones digging their children—and themselves—a bigger hole, complete with emotional baggage that makes it more difficult for their children to become organized, responsible, and accountable.

Creating the Positive Foundation

Parents often wonder why boys buy into my system so quickly; in two hours, I have the typical "impossible" teenager willing to give my organizational and time-management system a good try. The reason it works is that by simply *focusing on their strengths* instead of railing against what they are doing wrong, we set a foundation and build from there. It's demoralizing and ineffective to focus on the negative—who ever enjoyed that meeting with a boss who only told you everything you did wrong?

One of the main reasons my system works so well for boys is that they quickly find it to be the classic win–win situation. The truth is that when you help boys figure out what they truly desire and aspire to accomplish in their lives, (discussed in Chapter 4), you are finally giving them a real *reason* to become better organized and take control of their lives. Just getting good grades or being admitted to the right college are not enticing enough goals for most young people to embrace long-term changes to becoming a more invested, engaged, and active person. When you give boys the tools they need to organize their lives, not only do their grades improve but the overall quality of their lives also improves. By making study time better organized, boys feel less academic stress. When they get better grades and are more on top of their assignments, quizzes, and lunch, their relationship with their parents and teachers improves. As these boys learn to manage their time, they suddenly find that they have more time to devote to the things they truly love: hanging out with friends, playing video games, shooting hoops, and practicing with their band. Their parents are also less stressed because they no longer find themselves running down the driveway delivering the math homework that was due yesterday.

> By making study time better organized, boys feel less academic stress.

I frequently use the term *win–win* with students to discuss how becoming better organized and managing their time more effectively has countless benefits, with nearly no negative side effects. After all, what is so bad about learning how to do better in school while finding ways to have more free time? Classic win–win, and very convincing to preteen and teenage boys.

Have Cooperative Collaborative Meetings

Students who work with me quickly figure out that I am most interested in helping them find practical solutions that will empower them to reach their own personal potential. I offer suggestions and possible solutions, but it is ultimately the cooperative nature of our work that motivates the student to make changes. Similarly, I encourage you to use this book as a guide to come up with cooperative and collaborative solutions with your son. Have a family meeting or discussion (whatever works in your home with your family dynamic) where your child is able to vocalize his view of what he feels that he is struggling with, and you can all brainstorm solutions together, which can be incredibly powerful. *Note:* If you don't feel that your particular parent–child dynamic will make this sort of collaborative meeting successful, perhaps someone else close to your child (your spouse, family friend, mentor) might be the more appropriate choice.

You Are Not Alone: Seek Like-Minded Friends

My main office is located in a small town in the Silicon Valley, where there are about two degrees of separation between most people. Everyone knows—or knows of—everyone else. Maybe your community is like that or maybe it allows a certain level of anonymity. Even so, I often find myself consoling parents who think they're the only ones whose son doesn't turn in homework, has a GPA below a 3.0, or has a difficult time socially. Many of these parents know each other, and they often complain to me, confidentially, that they think their son is the only one. These same parents are friendly, go out to dinner socially, go on walks or play tennis together, run into each other at school events, and are family friends—but their fear of parenting failure keeps them from being honest with themselves and their friends—friends who could offer support, suggestions, and good humor.

If necessary, look outside your current crop of friends for like-minded support. While I was writing this book, I went to Sonoma, about an hour north of my home in San Francisco, hoping to write and have a relaxing time away. While I was there, a friend of mine who is a mother of three teenagers (two boys and a girl) invited me for a hike with a few of her friends. At first I hesitated, because I really needed to work, but then I figured that going on a nice hike with five mothers of teenagers could be considered "research," plus I never turn down the invitation for a brisk morning hike when the air is crisp and the incline is steep.

Along the way, these moms and I talked about college applications, teenage partying, teen pregnancy, and a host of other topics. These moms were real, refreshing, and warmhearted—but what struck me about these moms was that they were all honest and open about their kids' challenges and difficulties.

Later, my friend Laura, who had invited me on the hike, told me about how she had gotten to know each of the women on our hike. Laura had moved to Sonoma only a few years before when she and her husband built their dream house, and she spent her first few months in town feeling somewhat miserable.

"All the moms I met initially were pretending that everything was okay," she explained, "and that their kids were all perfect with no problems. Well, my kids are great kids, but they're not perfect and without problems. It took me a while to meet other mothers who were authentic and real about what they were going through."

Seeking authenticity and avoiding

Seeking authenticity and avoiding superficiality are important steps in creating a positive parental attitude that supports your son.

superficiality are important steps in creating a positive parental attitude that supports your son. Recognizing that there are issues that you are struggling with and finding other parents who have sons with similar challenges creates a sense of unity and understanding that can be crucial for improvement.

Avoid Competitive Parenting

Competitive parenting is a losing game. Even under the guise of being constructive, comparing notes with other parents can shift into a competition in a matter of moments, and it typically results in parents becoming anxious about where their son is (or isn't) with respect to his peers. You probably know who the competitive parent is in your neighborhood, and perhaps there is a bit of a competitive parent in all of us. Maybe your sister-in-law cannot stop talking about how her son is an absolute genius, and you are left wondering why your fourteen-year-old still forgets to tie his shoes most mornings.

One day last spring, I logged on to my computer to find a three-page, single-spaced email from Judy, a wonderful mother I'd known for years. I get these emails occasionally, and instead of replying and fueling the fire, I typically just pick up the phone. When I called her, she immediately recounted everything in her email: She was distressed about how her son, Evan, a high school sophomore, was probably behind in his college application process and how she woke up at 3:00 that morning worried about it.

"Judy, Evan's in good shape," I said, as reassuringly as I could. "His grades are going up, he's getting more confident and better organized, and he's doing a lot better than he was a year ago, don't you think?"

She agreed, but I could still hear the anxiety in her voice.

"Judy," I said, "can I ask you something? Did you run into anyone? Another parent, perhaps?"

Indeed she had, and had listened to breathless stories about how so-and-so didn't get into any of the schools he applied to even though he had a 4.3 GPA and a 2550 SAT score. At this point, I wanted to gently remind her that the SAT was only out of 2400 points, but I felt it would be a moot point.

The person she'd run into was Michael, a local father in town whom I have met peripherally but do not know well. I have fielded no fewer than fifteen emails from parents like Judy who'd had the misfortune to discuss parenting with Michael. No matter where Michael encounters another parent—the baseball bleachers, the grocery store, the soccer field—he takes it upon himself to helpfully dole out the misinformation he's gleaned in his efforts to get his son, Max, into the most competitive colleges.

Competitive parenting happens in all neighborhoods, with all parents, and is not helpful for anyone. I have often found that the most competitive parents are those who are unintentionally living vicariously through their child(ren). Competitive parenting undermines any efforts to create an environment in which children can feel successful because it creates unnecessary and inappropriate stress for everyone involved. Instead of focusing on their own son's personal gifts and strengths, parents wind up comparing his accomplishments to glorified stories of kids from around the block, a good deal of which are embellished, half-truths or simply lies. As a result, even the most well-intentioned parents don't always have their facts straight, so it's best to avoid the competitive parenting trap by diverting the subject or stopping the conversation altogether. Helping children grow up and become confident and comfortable with themselves and caring toward others is ultimately a far bigger accomplishment than any grade or score.

> Helping children grow up and become confident and comfortable with themselves and caring toward others is ultimately a far bigger accomplishment than any grade or score.

Bribery, Humiliation, and Negotiation Do Not Work

Sometimes parents come into my office and admit that they have given their child money for grades for years. After all, they tell me, school is really their "job," so why shouldn't they get paid for good grades? Oddly, they haven't realized that the bribing has clearly not been working because they are now in my office, desperate for help.

Bribery and negotiation—as well as their negative counterpart, humiliation—are detrimental and ineffective for many reasons. First and foremost, they give a value to scores and grades rather than to learning—and I cannot think of a faster way to promote cheating and other shortsighted behaviors. After all, if you are a fifteen-year-old boy who makes a good sum of money on every A, wouldn't that encourage you to do everything in your power to keep that cash flowing? These artificial reinforcements do not create happy, stable, and resilient individuals; instead, these children grow up to become dependent on outside props instead of personal motivation. Rather than figuring out what they enjoy and feel passionate about, they constantly focus on what will give them external rewards. These external rewards can also trigger an inflationary spiral because, like a gambler's fix, what might satiate your child today will likely be considered a pittance in a year or two.

Craig is an only child who lives with his grandparents on a large ranch. Craig's grandfather is a reserved and stoic businessman of considerable wealth; he is incredibly demanding and rigid in his care of Craig—it has obviously been many years since he had a teenager in his home, and I am not sure he played a huge role in the raising of his own children. Craig is a genuinely good kid with a warm heart and a hopeful disposition. Although he struggles to stay organized and focused on his academics for a variety of reasons, he does want to do well and gets frustrated with himself when he doesn't meet his own expectations or those of his grandfather.

Craig's grandfather made Craig a deal that he could have a new four-wheel-drive Ford F-150 truck as long as he maintained a 3.3 GPA. The minute his GPA went below a 3.3, the grandfather would take the keys away, no matter what—no excuses. Midway through his junior year, Craig came into my office panicked almost to the point of paralysis. He was struggling in his classes despite his genuine efforts, and he was mortified that his truck was going to be taken away. In addition to the pressure of school and his own serious life struggles, he was now dealing with the possible humiliation and loss of autonomy that would come with being unable to drive himself around. Instead of motivating him, this prospect paralyzed him, creating an overwhelming anxiety. He dropped all focus on learning and became scared of school—frightened that any mistake he made would lead to his truck being taken away.

It's rare, but sometimes I have the unfortunate scene in my office when a parent—usually someone new to working with me—begins to list the various failures of their son in front of me, sometimes even berating him, and it's clear that this is a common scene for them. Believe me, very little in an adolescent's life is more humiliating than a public dressing-down, particularly in front of someone he has just met. No kid gets the slightest amount of motivation from being convinced that others find him second-rate simply because he makes the normal mistakes of growing up.

> No kid gets the slightest amount of motivation from being convinced that others find him second-rate simply because he makes the normal mistakes of growing up.

To help your child grow and develop as a student and a person, he needs to feel comfortable making mistakes and growing within his own abilities. By bribing him, you are setting the bar where you think it should be instead of allowing him to develop the intrinsic motivation that, who knows, could likely have him one day exceeding your wildest expectations. By humiliating him, you're telling him that mistakes and failure are synonymous; they're not. If they were, we'd all be getting Fs every day of our lives.

Your Son *Does* Care (He Just May Not Want You to Know It)

Sometimes a parent will call me, terrified about his or her son's grades and proceed to tell me that the child, on the other hand, is perfectly fine with the situation. Like Gus, the Seemingly Satisfied Underachiever you'll meet in the next chapter, this boy doesn't seem to care at all that he's just barely passing his classes. Nothing the parent says seems to have any effect.

I tell these parents that their son is trying to live up to five million different expectations, including his own, and that the influence of his peers, teachers, school counselors, coaches, parents, and the media can be overwhelming. Many boys already feel that they are not living up to the spoken or unspoken expectations of where they should be, want to be, or could be. Developmentally, boys are already dealing with their own questions of, *Why can't I do this?* that they often do not share with their parents, so for their parents now to say, *Why can't he do this?* can be remarkably debilitating. For many boys, trying to meet these seemingly unattainable expectations leads to an overwhelming anxiety and causes them to shut down and act as though they don't care. After all, it's easier to seem ambivalent than to appear vulnerable.

Imagine you have a boss who always gets under your skin. No matter what you do, it is never good enough or it could have been better or different—there is always some complaint or some way you could have been or should have been. After a while, you would probably shut down too or find a way to leave the company and work for a more inspiring boss!

> Support and encourage your son to develop useful systems and ideas rather than demeaning and criticizing his past performance.

Drop the preconceived notions of what you think your son should be or could be—because boys already place enormous pressure on themselves. Support and encourage your son to develop useful systems and ideas rather than demeaning and criticizing his past performance. Most parents rarely realize that their own preconceived notions can have a huge impact on their child's emotional health and self-esteem.

Make a Fresh Start and Just Let It Go

A few years back, a wonderful mother named Jill called me, beside herself with concern about her son, William, who was struggling with the new academic requirements as a freshman in high school. He had gone to parochial school up until the eighth grade and was starting high school at the large, local public school near his house. He really hadn't made too many friends, and besides being peripherally involved in a few activities, he spent most of his time at home. I had first met William just months before, when he took part in an organizational workshop I offer to incoming high school students. I remembered him clearly because when he was sitting at a table with another young boy, he stretched out his hand and said, politely and welcomingly, "Hi, I'm William. I haven't met you yet." The other boy took his hand limply, not knowing exactly what to do and awkwardly introduced himself.

I immediately sensed that William was and is a natural leader and a kind and considerate person whose moral compass and wisdom were beyond his years. He is the kind of student who peers look up to and admire, and the kind of person I could see being a respected political leader or running a company someday. Sounds like a great kid, right? Why would he ever need my help? Well, organizationally he was a bit of a mess.

Instead of recognizing her son's talents and strengths, Jill was overwhelmed by the things that he was struggling with—finding a group of friends, having a social life that satisfied him, and struggling in honors classes that were probably not best suited for him. Because of this distraction, she had a hard time realizing the importance of his strengths: his solid moral character, his integrity, and his genuine openness and warmth. Over the next several months, William and I worked together to improve his organizational habits and come up with some goals. He mentioned running for student government and, after much encouragement, did so and won. Two years later, he was a school leader and scholar-athlete, a young man who the principal has speak on behalf of the high school at functions within the community.

One of the most important things you can do while reading this book and following the tips is to look at it as a fresh start. Whatever makes you angry or frustrated about your child's past academic performance—let it go. Stop complaining about your children. Take the crucial first step to helping your son become more engaged in his learning process by letting go of past disappointments, expectations, and challenges.

> Whatever is making you angry or frustrated about your child's past academic performance—let it go.

Try this exercise: Take out a piece of paper and write down an incident involving your son's disorganization that irritated or frustrated you (if you experienced both emotions from one situation, bonus points!). What exactly about the situation angered you most? How did you react to it? Did your reaction help or hurt the situation? How did your son respond to your reaction? Did your reaction increase or decrease the stress your son feels about being disorganized? Did it make him feel more or less overwhelmed?

You might want to save this piece of paper and look at it again after you've chased that school bus one more time (no changes, even positive ones, come immediately).

Accept Your Child for Who He Really Is

Years ago, I worked with Nick, who is described as a Creative Wonder in Chapter 3. Nick is a really cool, fun kid—spontaneous, energetic, and lively, he lights up a room with his big smile and oversize personality. He loves music and played in two bands at school as well as in his own punk rock band that performed locally about once a month. Music was his passion. His father, Roger, a conservative and dignified attorney, had a difficult time understanding Nick—their personalities were completely different, and Roger could not understand why Nick was not neater, more punctual, and better organized.

Roger made it clear that he felt that Nick was generally underperforming and not living up to expectations. Each time he did that, Nick would retreat even further, becoming so overwhelmed by the prospect of failing that he would just completely shut down. Roger and Nick's communication completely broke down, in part because Roger could never realize that Nick desperately wanted to live up to his dad's expectations of him and feared that he never would. Roger didn't realize that boys have an incredible desire to live up to expectations— especially the expectations of their father or other male figure.

Every time Nick struggled with something or had a less than ideal outcome, Roger would say something like, "You always do that! Why can't you ever learn?!" and with that, Nick would feel even worse about the situation. Despite their differences and Nick's outward nonchalance, Nick wanted to be validated for his efforts and his strengths, and Roger became frustrated when it appeared that Nick did not care.

Who is your son? What are his talents and gifts? What does he truly enjoy? Think about that and reflect for a moment—we often overlook those gifts when we are staring at low academic grades and scores. Look at your son as a young person who can really make a difference in whatever passion he chooses to pursue. By focusing on the positive, you can change the framework with which you approach his organizational and time-management habits and then help him start to take steps to create a successful transition for himself.

These days, it seems, many parents operate under the fear that if their kid messes up with bad grades, low test scores, or teenage mischief, there will be no college, no future, no job, no spouse or family, and he will still be parked on their couch at age forty-five playing the newest version of Halo. As a result, we no longer let kids make mistakes; we shield them from the life-affirming growing experiences that come from accepting the consequences of their own choices and figuring out their own individual path.

Remember Diane and Scott, the over-involved, hyper-organized mom and her son described at the beginning of this chapter? Diane eventually realized that her hovering was preventing her from achieving her ultimate goal of letting Scott grow and develop his own set of skills. She also realized that by dropping his lunch and missing materials off every day, she was enabling his disorganized behavior, and so she let him face the consequences of forgetting an assignment or two or not having lunch, which made him more cognizant (not right away, but in time) of needing to take ownership of his own responsibilities.

Let Him Take Ownership of His Successes and Mistakes

From his freshman to senior year, Diane stepped back and let Scott grow into his own young person, developing his own skills and facing his own challenges. Some weeks and months were smoother than others, but by the time he reached his senior year, he was a reliable, competent, and hardworking young man who wrote in his planner most days and turned in his homework without his mother's help. He is currently a successful college student.

Remain Positive and It Will Happen

I have seen hundreds of boys completely transform their lives, and most of these transformations were the results of hours, weeks, months, and even years of work. It is a progression, not a sprint. Like most long-lasting changes, the evolution of changes with a boy is incremental and takes time; sometimes when a boy takes four steps forward, he seemingly jumps two steps back. But that is okay, because he is on his own journey and is making progress in his own time. Remaining optimistic—even when things look bleak—is the key.

> Remaining optimistic—even when things look bleak—is the key.

About half the boys I work with are like Joey. He was a high school sophomore when we first met, slightly awkward physically and socially; he was a very nice and kind young person but still trying to figure out his place in and out of school. The first semester we worked together was, quite simply, like pulling teeth. Joey understood the habits and adopted half of them and then forgot the others, or one week he had fully organized his binders only to find them in complete disarray the following week. At some points, I could see his mom's jaw clench when she saw him slipping on the habits and making mistakes, but I convinced her to remain positive.

"It doesn't happen overnight," I explained. "Just when you think they will never get it . . . magic."

It's true—at some point it just clicks. That first semester, Joey found himself mid-semester with three Ds and an F. Through it all, I remained optimistic and focused on the habits with him, starting slowly to pick up the pieces where we could and starting over when we needed to start over. That first semester, Joey crawled to the finish line and didn't make huge improvements over his past academic performance. He started to understand what he needed to do, and the next semester was a completely different story.

Because his family moved, he was no longer working with me directly, but he knew the habits and had the goals. At the end of the first marking period, I got an ecstatic email from his mother, telling me that he seemed to have figured out what he needed to do to get where he wanted to go. She attached a copy of his first-semester grades:

Chemistry: A–
Spanish: B–
P.E.: A
Algebra II: B
U.S. History: A
English: A
Art: A

In her email, Joey's mom wrote that she could really see that "he is finally proud of himself," one of the best motivators a young person today can have. It is sometimes six months to a year after boys are introduced to these strategies that they start to see dramatic, monumental success as Joey did. In the upcoming chapters, I outline the organizational tips and strategies that have worked for many preteen and teenage students, but this book is about the whole picture, not just organizing and managing time. As a parent, your role is to remain positive throughout the journey and realize that it is all about your son's progress and your support of that progress.

Summary

It's natural to feel that bringing a new structure into your child's life will mean more work for everybody, but in fact the reverse is true. The organizational and time-management techniques in this book actually lead to *better* academic results with *less* overall anxiety and effort—and that's an important thing to mention when presenting these materials to your child. It's also good for you to realize that both you and your child have enough stresses in your lives, and there's no reason to add more by harping on his shortcomings or comparing his academic progress to his peers'. This is not to say that you can't find other parents who share a positive philosophy about leading balanced and affirmative lives—you absolutely should. Just remember that at the end of the day, your family's unique challenges and particular strengths will determine how you move forward and how you will measure success. This book won't change who your child is, but it can help you move aside those obstacles preventing him from being the successful student and young person he wants to be.

3

Identifying Your Son's (Dis)organizational Style

Each student who walks into my office is unique in his or her strengths, gifts, and challenges. Some students struggle mainly with organization, while others appear supremely organized with respect to their binders and backpacks but can never seem to get assignments in on time or figure out how to do anything before the last minute. Others make all the right decisions about organization but find themselves struggling and anxious during tests.

Just as there are many different ways of describing methods of organization (left-brained or right-brained, a pack rat or a pile person), there are also styles of *disorganization* that are quite distinct and quite recognizable after you've helped hundreds of students work through these challenges, as I have. You might find that your son has characteristics and traits of one or several of the different styles I describe in this chapter and throughout the book. This insight will help you guide him to solutions and strategies that will work for him during his academic career and beyond.

One of the reasons I've been able to help students with issues ranging from chronic disorganization to significant executive functioning disabilities is that, while the overall tenets of the system are consistent, the components allow for a certain degree of adaptability and flexibility in helping boys create a system that works for them. Above all, the most important part of my work is helping each young person to come away with a sense of control and greater confidence about his opportunities and more hope about what he can accomplish.

The examples I'll use for the rest of this chapter are composites of real students I've worked with. The anecdotes are all true, but they are also representative. In other words, I hope that you'll recognize your son in one or more of them. I'll return to these archetypes again and again in the following chapters.

The Over-Scheduled Procrastinator

Tim, a typical Over-Scheduled Procrastinator, is a natural leader, with a warm smile and wry sense of humor. Senior class president and a member of the varsity tennis team, he takes several honors and AP classes and is well liked and well respected by peers and faculty alike. He's naturally engaging and maintains an active social life, including a group of friends he's known since elementary school. At school, he spends his time between classes and at lunch running student council meetings, hanging out with his friends on the quad, or playing intramural sports. When there's a social activity, special occasion, or school community project, you can bet the Over-Scheduled Procrastinator is involved, if not in charge. Although to

> Although to the outside world he seems to have it all together, his internal life is actually one of nearly debilitating stress.

the outside world he seems to have it all together, his internal life is actually one of nearly debilitating stress.

You see, Tim is an incredibly hard worker, but he's consumed by his commitments. He's constantly juggling a full load of schoolwork alongside the dozens of text messages, phone calls, and emails about the upcoming winter dance, the school rally, and a friend's weekend birthday party. Because he is so busy and engaged so intricately within his school community (in so many great ways), he is always balancing too many activities. He's unable to look at the big picture and make plans in advance or figure out which activities he's doing out of a sense of obligation rather than personal fulfillment. He can never manage to see any of his teachers for extra help, as much as he would like to, because there are four other things he has to attend to first and the bell always rings before he gets to the teacher's classroom. As a result, he becomes easily overwhelmed and often feels like he is in a desperate struggle just to keep up.

Academically, Tim does fine. He never forgets to do assignments and generally turns things in on time, but because he's a very typical procrastinator, Tim's study cycle often centers on a looming deadline—a long-avoided project due date or upcoming test. The evening before this deadline involves many wasted hours of unfocused agitation until, after midnight, exhausted and sleep deprived, Tim settles into the task. As difficult as this routine is emotionally, it's also hard on him physically, leaving him susceptible to ugly colds and flu and general weary crankiness. But it is the way he has worked for years, and before coming into my office, he would just repeat the cycle for each upcoming test or project.

For Tim and other Over-Scheduled Procrastinators, the key is creating a strategy of planning ahead, managing time, and tackling assignments without distractions, as discussed in detail in Chapter 5. And because the Over-Scheduled Procrastinator is always going a mile a minute, it's just as important to build in opportunities to rest and relax.

Traits of an Over-Scheduled Procrastinator

- Maintains involvement in school, athletics, community, and/or friendships

- Works hard, is motivated to do well academically

- Is a sociable, likable, natural leader with a wide social network

- Believes that because of his many time commitments, he can't start projects until the last minute

- Tries to manage multiple tasks, but has to redo or backtrack because he often loses things, forgets to write down his homework, or becomes scattered because he is juggling too much

- Becomes irritable and shuts down at deadlines, and will start a big project at 11:00 the night before it's due

- Tends to overcommit without thinking through the consequences and becomes easily stressed or overwhelmed

The Scattered Charmer

Scott is a happy-go-lucky kid who's funny and fun to be around and doesn't seem to stress about anything (often to the chagrin of his parents and teachers). Nothing seems too important or serious, and there is rarely any sense of urgency regarding his schoolwork, tests, quizzes, and projects. He has a laid-back, nothing-is-that-big-a-deal personality, and he is the type of kid who will walk out the door with only half of what he needs that day, leaving the rest scattered throughout his room or sitting on the printer. Most mornings his mother lunges out the front door after him, handing him his lunch, his English essay, and the soccer uniform he was supposed to have returned the week before.

Because Scott is a naturally gifted test taker, scoring well on standardized tests, his parents initially had high expectations for success in high school. In elementary and middle school Scott was often able to use his smile and his charm to finagle his way out of missteps. But now, in high school, he often misses points for not following directions properly, turning in homework late (with a smile!), or failing to turn in all the parts of a project at once. At school, Charmers spend any and all time out of class socializing and generally creating harmless mischief. There is rarely any sense of urgency with Scott—which, while refreshing, can be troubling when he has a paper due on Monday and is spending most of Sunday figuring out how to download the newest episode of *24* to his iPhone. As with many Scattered Charmers, Scott outwardly seems like he does not really care whether or not he does well in school—most parents and teachers initially think that boys like Scott are unmotivated and apathetic toward school. However, their outwardly laid-back appearance masks a very real inner frustration. When Scott gets to the point at which this stress becomes overwhelming, I can almost see the steam coming out of his ears.

Boys like Scott simply don't know how to become organized or create a system that would work (because nobody has ever shown them one), and that leads to trouble being consistent and following through on good intentions. In addition, some Charmers

> However, their outwardly laid-back appearance masks a very real inner frustration.

are bored in the static classroom setting, whereas they thrive in environments that allow for social interaction and group activities. Some Charmers are in need of a challenge or a way to feel engaged and may not yet have found anything they are interested in pursuing on an ongoing basis.

Traits of a Scattered Charmer
- Is easygoing, funny, outwardly calm
- Becomes forgetful, somewhat messy, easily distracted by social obligations

- Engaged socially and well known among peers

- Thrives in social settings, can be bored in school

- Finds it difficult to prioritize, rarely has any sense of urgency

- Starts homework after the social and the extracurricular activities have ended

- Tests well—often has high standardized test scores and lower than average grades

- Has a difficult time setting aside time for his work—something is always more important

- Misses easy assignments, forgets about tests, and often loses points when he fails to follow directions

The Tech Master

A wunderkind with computers and setting up complex surround-sound systems, Peter is enamored with technology. He loves anything and everything technology-related—computers, phones, video games—and is always current on the latest and greatest. When Peter becomes enthralled with a project, his level of dedication is unparalleled. He can spend hours in the garage taking something apart and trying to figure out how to put it back together, usually succeeding and actually making improvements in the process. He rushes to finish his homework so he can start playing *World of Warcraft* or whatever gaming system he is currently dedicated to, and is a really intelligent and strategic thinker.

Not as outwardly social as Scott and Tim, Peter uses his computer and the text messaging on his phone as his main forms of socialization (and distraction!). He is much more comfortable having a conversation over IM than face-to-face or over the phone, and his witty and irreverent nature comes through mainly in his computer conversations. He cannot resist checking his email fifty times in a two-hour period, and because he's tweaked his computer (or cell phone or PDA) to make a sound whenever he gets an email or someone posts something on his Facebook page, the result is almost thirty *pings* per hour; and he regularly stops what he's doing to check what has happened.

Peter's parents, on the other hand, view this commitment to technology as something bordering on addiction and would like him to unplug and come out of his room once in a while. They're worried that his fascination with the virtual world distracts him from real life, and Peter's general response is that he needs his computer to do his homework properly, even though the work takes a backseat to the technology itself. He sees nothing wrong with a five-to-one ratio of Xbox to homework, which is generally (to him) rote and boring.

Like many Tech Masters, Peter is quite intelligent and grasps concepts at a much more complex level than his peer group. His test-taking ability is off the charts, but he often misses points by forgetting to turn in the easy assignments because he thinks they are no big deal. His binders are in complete disarray, and he never uses his planner. If he gets really interested in an assignment, however, he will put forth a monumental effort, lose track of time, and become frustrated at the mediocre results he gets from his all-or-nothing attempts at academic success. For Peter, figuring out how to use technology as an aid and not a distraction—using the computer for word processing without turning on the instant messenger, for instance—is one of his most important steps toward becoming better at managing his time effectively and efficiently.

> His test-taking ability is off the charts, but he often misses points by forgetting to turn in the easy assignments because he thinks they are no big deal.

Traits of a Tech Master

- Loves computers, gadgets, and all sorts of modern technology

- Spends a lot of time indoors

- Uses the computer as his main form of communication and distraction; uses the computer as his social crutch

- Is often shy and less bold in face-to-face conversations

- Easily enthralled with technology—insists that he always needs technology to complete his homework

- Becomes deeply invested (be that a project, video game, or even, rarely, schoolwork) when he becomes really interested in something

- Has great conceptual abilities and often thinks about complex intellectual processes, can be very creative and possesses much higher-level thinking than his peers

- Forgets assignments, is incredibly messy and distracted, and fails to turn in assignments that he has deemed worthless

The Seriously Struggling Student

Paul's backpack is always fairly neat. He's good about using his planner and has a system in place for organizing his binders. There may be a few straggling pieces of paper here and there, but overall he's fairly organized—much more so than the typical seventh grade boy who walks in to see me. Paul's mom told me that he was excited to come and see me and was prepared to grasp whatever organizational and time-management strategies I could give him.

At home and school, Paul is diligent and good-natured. A concrete thinker, he doesn't let himself get caught up in extrapolations from the information presented to him. He never misses a homework assignment, does everything to the best of his ability, and really *wants* to do well. At school, he is consistently at the teacher's office hours, and most of his teachers remark that he is a pleasure to have in class—a quiet and attentive student. He has a select group of friends, but struggles with his academic and personal self-confidence and self-esteem. Despite his efforts, Paul has always been a Struggling Student. His processing speed was tested to be in the 13th percentile, and it takes him hours to complete the reading assignments his classmates finish in less than thirty minutes. He qualifies for extended time on class exams and standardized tests but is too embarrassed to use it because he doesn't want to be labeled as dumb—his word—by his peers. At school, he hangs back with a small group of friends and doesn't really venture outside his social circle. He quietly belongs to a few clubs, but has yet to find his niche.

> He qualifies for extended time on class exams and standardized tests but is too embarrassed to use it because he doesn't want to be labeled as dumb—his word—by his peers.

As a Struggling Student, he scores poorly on standardized tests and sometimes gets frustrated and overwhelmed by his inability to understand concepts that he feels his peers understand more readily. Paul's confidence in his academic abilities is pretty low, and the lack of success in the classroom is beginning to affect this polite, punctual, and motivated kid's self-esteem.

In addition to using study strategies that could help him learn material more effectively and decrease the overall amount of time he spends studying, it's really important for Paul to explore some arenas where he can find success and validation outside of the classroom. Whether that is through volunteering with children or the elderly, trying a new athletic endeavor, or taking up a musical instrument or other lessons, one of the most crucial things for Paul is that he finds an avenue where he can discover personal success through developing a passion.

Traits of a Seriously Struggling Student

- Has a difficult time in school, struggles to keep up with his peers academically

- Takes a long time with homework and reading assignments

- Diligently gets work done—turns in all homework but gets low grades on tests even after he studies extensively

- Struggles with low academic self-confidence and self-esteem

- Embarrassed by his struggles and rarely asks questions or participates in class

- Thinks concretely—will do exactly what is asked of him without questioning authority

- Wants to please—polite, pleasant, and well-meaning; motivated to do well but academic challenges sometimes overwhelm him

- May have a diagnosed learning disability or challenges

The Creative Wonder

Nick, a high school sophomore, is an intensely talented singer and guitarist who dreams of one day making it big in the record industry. He and I often joke that he needs to save me a few tickets, because one day his tours will be all sold out. Students like Nick—whom I like to call Creative Wonders—are usually intensely talented in music, studio arts, or dramatic arts. They are wildly artistic and likely to favor the right side of their brain, although in class they can seem scattered and deep in thought or reflection. They can often be caught doodling or even working on outside projects when they're supposed to be paying attention to a lecture.

Creative Wonders tend to concentrate completely on their artistic endeavors, to the point where they get lost in the details of a project and fail to surface to deal with day-to-day issues. They also have a hard time designing and managing their own concrete strategies for organization because most of the techniques they come up with don't fit their natural style of learning and retaining information. When Nick and I first started working together, I immediately sensed that he was perceptive and sensitive to the world around him at a much greater level than some of his peers. His creative writing assignment for his English class had levels of humor and depth far beyond his sophomore peers, and yet his grades would make one mistakenly think he was a sub-par student.

> Creative Wonders tend to concentrate completely on their artistic endeavors, to the point where they get lost in the details of a project and fail to surface to deal with day-to-day issues.

When we checked his backpack I found his binders were completely intact, filled with paper that was neat and perfectly hole-punched but, unfortunately, blank. Underneath the binders was an overwhelming pile of papers crumpled into the bottom of his backpack.

Nick's struggle with time management is exacerbated by the fact that many of his artistic endeavors—such as the music he writes for his band and his band's local concert performances—can take great periods of time to create and develop. This commitment takes a toll; when he finally gets around to his homework he often finds it boring, unimportant, irrelevant to his life, or all of the above. As an abstract thinker, he questions why he needs to complete tasks that seem trivial to his own personal growth and development.

Creative Wonders like Nick need a regular outlet to pursue their creative interests, preferably within the classroom setting as well as outside. Meaningful work is important to him, and he needs to be actively engaged in what he is doing, otherwise he finds it pointless. It is also through creative work that he becomes more motivated to find some level of organization and success with time management, if for no other reason than to have enough *time* to lead the meaningful life he craves. In addition, finding ways for creative pursuits to be a part of the academic arena can be effective in helping a Creative Wonder become more motivated. But organization remains a constant struggle for him and he often has to regroup and reorganize to get himself back on track. Good strategies for the Creative Wonder include frequent breaks to help avoid the frustration of what seems like mundane work and to make sure something that he is passionate about is part of his daily life. Incorporating his creative pursuits within his academic setting whenever possible will also help a Creative Wonder become more motivated within the classroom environment.

Traits of a Creative Wonder

- Creatively intuitive; perceptive, abstract thinker

- Gets lost in the details; has a difficult time seeing the bigger picture

- Spends hours on a project, focusing on minute details, all the while forgetting about simple homework assignments that are due the next day

- Engages in the pursuit of his interests, but avoids completing those that seem mundane or rote

- Seems scattered, messy, with things all over the place and often misplaced and crumpled

- Intricate doodler and daydreamer, often forgets to write down assignments in class

- Needs frequent breaks when completing homework because he can easily become distracted from completing routine homework tasks

The Intellectual Conversationalist

A member of his high school's varsity debate team, Clay is an intellectual's intellectual. He is incredibly verbal, a deep thinker and analyzer, and noticeably more advanced than many of his classmates. Clay loves talking with teachers and other adults and finds validation in his ability to participate in class and offer pithy analysis and insight. When he raises his hand, some of his classmates wince because they won't understand half of what he will say, and the other half will be something they would never even have considered. If you were to survey his classmates, they would deem him to be "one of the smartest people in the class."

He spends all his free time with his debating friends, often at weekend-long tournaments and strategy sessions. He can spend hours creating the perfect case or argument and works diligently to prepare for tournaments and improve his speaking style. Debate is his passion, and he can convince anyone of anything, but he's often unable to filter his ideas succinctly and logically, as though he had *so many* ideas and wants to blurt them all out at once instead of just offering what would be appropriate.

Like most Intellectual Conversationalists, Clay's thoughts are complex and challenging; however, Clay remains in the bottom half of his class academically. He struggles on tests and quizzes—particularly in math and science—because he lacks any semblance of study skills and does not even know where to begin. His room looks like several tornadoes hit it *simultaneously*, and he can barely find his shoes before walking out the door with a pile of papers stuffed into his backpack. He forgets assign-

> Like most Intellectual Conversationalists, Clay's thoughts are complex and challenging; however, Clay remains in the bottom half of his class academically.

ments, turns in others on crumpled paper, and will sometimes have to wake up early to write an English paper that was assigned two weeks before. He is also unable to recognize when he needs to prioritize and focus on something other than debate.

Because of his sub-par grades, he has been unable to pass into some of the advanced history and English classes, where he would feel intellectually comfortable and be appropriately challenged. He has some marked difficulty recognizing and admitting that his strategies for managing his schoolwork aren't really working for him. He is not one to openly ask for help or admit that he is not doing well—which is one of the reasons his classmates mistakenly think he is going to be their valedictorian.

Clay's main challenge is that he needs to create time and space for doing his homework proactively rather than reactively (see Chapter 4). Unfortunately, Clay is confident that he's at the top of his game—Intellectual Conversationalists tend to think they're always right—and constantly questions any attempts to alter his behavior. A good technique to use with a boy like Clay is to make it seem like his idea or to use examples from his other interests—debate prep, for instance—to show him how organization can help him become even more successful at whatever endeavor he deems worthwhile.

Traits of an Intellectual Conversationalist

- Participates actively; very verbal in class

- Recognized by his peers as being incredibly intellectual

- Interacts easily with adults, has a greater challenge with peers who may not fully understand his elevated thought process

- Struggles with basic organization—doesn't use a planner, has crumpled papers at the bottom of his backpack; binders are nonexistent or empty

- Becomes enthralled in projects that he is excited about and loses track of time

- Has a tough time admitting when he needs help or that his system of organization is not working

- Has difficulty prioritizing, can be stubborn

The Sincere Slacker

Most Sincere Slackers come into my office baffled as to why they are not doing as well as they would like to; they're convinced they're making monumental, supreme efforts to be successful in school, and yet they fail to see tangible results. They think that spending a half hour on a five-paragraph essay is a lot because, hey, thirty minutes is more than zero and at least it's typed, right? They're truly confused as to why they're working so hard but not seeing the real results their friends do and are completely clueless as to what's needed to be successful in completing homework, studying for tests and quizzes, and putting together long-term projects.

Like most Sincere Slackers, Damian lacks reasonable study expectations and the structures to support them. The front pockets of Damian's binder are clean because he stuffs all the important papers in the bottom of his backpack, where they eventually disintegrate. He makes three flash cards covering five chapters two days before the history test and thinks he's fully prepared. In addition, he has no idea how to manage his time efficiently or effectively. He happily spends hours socializing on the computer before even opening his book for the chapter test the next day—the one on the information he barely understood in class but was hesitant to ask questions about.

Most Sincere Slackers will not pretend to be proud of their performance, but they don't see their struggles as self-inflicted. They've gotten it into their head that there's a mystical secret to academic success, and they just didn't get the memo. Many Sincere Slackers are on the shy side and tend not to speak up or ask questions for clarification. They are not very involved in outside activities, and if they are in a club or team, they are more of a peripheral member and rarely step up to a leadership role. The lack of confidence they feel from their academic struggles tends also to make them doubt their personal abilities in other areas of their life. They're also the ones who find themselves in the final minutes of the semester scrambling to finish assignments long overdue and who make up missing projects for the teacher who will throw them a few extra points so they can pass the class.

> They've gotten it into their head that there's a mystical secret to academic success, and they just didn't get the memo.

Your Sincere Slacker may initially balk when you explain what habits he needs to change to see the results he aspires to; surely this is a ridiculous amount of work? For Damian, it was really important that he avoid becoming overwhelmed, so I showed him a few strategies at a time rather than all at once. The challenge was getting him to give it a shot for a few weeks, using the strategies I outline in the following chapters. Once he saw his initial success and that he could, in fact, achieve his academic goals, he became much more engaged and raised the bar for himself to levels that his parents, teachers, and peers had never imagined.

Traits of a Sincere Slacker

- Thinks he is working diligently when his effort is actually far less than what is needed for success

- Completes tasks for the most part, but often lets some assignments slip through the cracks

- Becomes confused as to why he is not doing well

- Creates the illusion (for both himself and others!) that he is working hard—spends hours in his room doing his homework, even though he is ineffectively toggling between his homework, instant messenger, cell phone texts, and the Internet

- Has few, if any, areas in which he seems actively engaged or passionate

- Misunderstands the amount of effort required to get a large assignment or project done; waits until the last minute and puts in minimal effort

- Focuses on quantity (getting the assignment done) over quality (putting in a substantial effort)

The Seemingly Satisfied Underachiever

When Gus first walked into my office, he seemed fine with the fact that he was getting Cs and Ds in his classes, his only annoyance that he might have to spend some of his summer vacation in school to make up for his dismal performance. Even though he was capable of greater achievements, like Damian, the Slacker, Gus never really learned what it took to achieve his full potential and never figured out how much effort it took to succeed—or if he *did* learn, he didn't seem to care too much.

Gus was an expert at weaving a story of success to his parents, teachers, and peers. He was a great talker, incredibly verbal—for lack of a better term, the ultimate bullshit artist. Each semester, he vowed to his parents that he was starting with a clean slate and that this semester he was doing *great*! He would concoct elaborate stories of how he was always going to see the teacher for extra help, his homework was all done in advance, and he was doing really well and felt confident in all his classes. He proudly boasted that he aced all his tests—

only for his parents to find out from a progress report or a phone call home that he had eight missing homework assignments and had never once seen any of his teachers outside of class. Oh, and those tests he said he aced? Gus failed most of them and got Ds on the others.

Initially, dealing with Gus's schoolwork shenanigans had his parents concerned that they had raised a pathological liar, but the truth was that he was making up the lies to make his parents happy and tell them what they wanted to hear. He created this false sense of reality to escape the fact that he really did not have a clue as to what was going on and he felt absolutely worthless about it. Even though he was telling his parents that he was seeing his teachers for extra help, Gus was frightened to go in and reveal to them how completely clueless he was.

Gus actually had quite a few deep interests—none of them were school related—and that was fine, except that his school performance was making him doubt his own personal abilities and potential for self-improvement. Most of his peers, teachers, and even his parents had written him off and figured that he just didn't care about doing well or pursuing his own personal potential. They were completely incorrect. In Gus's case, it took just one teacher to notice Gus's strength—it turned out he was quite a talented writer—and offer sincere and genuine praise and encouragement.

> Most of his peers, teachers, and even his parents had written him off and figured that he just didn't care about doing well or pursuing his own personal potential.

Seemingly Satisfied Underachievers are sometimes the toughest students to engage in the process of getting organized and managing their time more effectively. Because they have spent so long concocting this false reality for themselves, they need to be able to admit their fears and frustrations before they can ever move forward—essentially, they need to start to understand that it is okay to seek help. They need help to visualize their future plans, dreams, and pursuits, and they need help to redefine their idea of themselves—this is crucial for them to create the space to start believing in their abilities. With that help, Seemingly Satisfied Underachievers can begin to see that fairly small concrete changes can potentially make a big impact on their opportunities and that it's never too late for a fresh start.

Traits of a Seemingly Satisfied Underachiever

- Seems like he does not care about school

- Talks with adults very easily, articulate conversationalist

- Characterizes himself as a low performer

- Weaves intricate stories of academic effort and success and seems in control of his schoolwork, but parents find out his reports represent a false reality

- Puts in minimal effort for school assignments or does not bother to complete them at all

- Seems unengaged and unmotivated by school

Chances are, one or more of these organizational styles resonates with you—perhaps your son is a bit of a Sincere Slacker as well as a Creative Wonder, with a smidgeon of Tech Master in there (he loves video games, is heavily invested in his live-action role-playing troupe but doesn't quite understand why his fifteen minutes of homework time isn't cutting it). This book is designed to give you strategies to help your son create an organizational and time-management plan that works with his particular needs and his own personal style. Throughout the book, I will offer tips that are specific to certain organizational styles as well as an overarching plan that covers time, space, organization, and study skills—so, take a deep breath, visualize success, think positively, and let's begin!

Summary

Nobody likes labels, but sometimes it's useful to give names to groups of traits if only to help identify problems.

- The Over-Scheduled Procrastinator seems to have the world at his feet but can never seem to get ahead, meet a deadline without a major meltdown, or turn down another social commitment.

- The Scattered Charmer does okay academically, but at a cost because his forgetfulness and general laissez-faire attitude means you're spending far too much time dropping off forgotten homework assignments or hunting up study sheets.

- Tech Masters can easily show you how to program your iPhone or keep the household network up and running, but they're much less successful putting those technological temptations aside to buckle down and study.

- The Seriously Struggling Student would love to be a master at anything; unfortunately, his lower-than-average processing speeds make even a normal academic workload a challenge and any distraction puts him even farther in the hole.

- Your typical Creative Wonder is a genius at the keyboard, easel, or lens but is in serious need of a workable plan to succeed within the school walls.

- Intellectual Conversationalists excel in the language arts but somehow can't bring that same level of mastery to the written assignment or test (and can't for the life of them understand why).

- The Sincere Slacker has convinced himself that a little effort in just the right place is sufficient and is genuinely puzzled at the lackluster results of this academic philosophy.

- The Sincere Slacker's counterpart—the Seemingly Satisfied Underachiever—puts in the same modicum of effort but has no problem with this less-than-stellar result. After all, it's just *school*, right?

4

Setting Academic and Personal Goals

The first time students come into my office, we spend the initial few hours organizing their binders, going through their planner, and filing away any papers that are at the bottom of their backpack. As we organize, I ask them about activities they enjoy and things they want to accomplish, and I try to get a sense of their interests and passions. Far too often, we adults tend to overlook those things that make a young person feel happy and fulfilled; instead, we focus solely on problems—what's *not* going well in school in relation to homework, tests, and GPAs. Often students are surprised that I'm so interested in what they love to do—they thought they were just coming in to learn how to get organized—and they can get quite excited talking about their rock band or love of rowing or how much they really enjoy reading historical fiction.

> Far too often, we adults tend to overlook those things that make a young person feel happy and fulfilled; instead, we focus solely on problems—what's *not* going well in school in relation to homework, tests, and GPAs.

Once I've learned about their individual interests, I explain how they can more efficiently get their homework and studying done by adopting organizational and time-management skills so that they have more time to pursue those very passions. Then, before they leave, I have them come up with three academic and three personal goals that they want to accomplish within the next semester or school year. In coming up with these goals, students are taking two very important steps: They're establishing a clear purpose and path for accomplishing what *they* want to accomplish, and they're beginning to view being *organized* as an important part of finding their own personal pathway.

I concentrate on personal interests because much of our educational system today has unintentionally created a structure in which we focus on the results rather than the process. That is, we force kids to do things—memorize or learn facts and go through the motions—without asking where their passions lie and helping them cultivate those individual talents. As a result, many students quickly become disengaged and lose interest. By enabling your son to set goals and envision his pursuit of his own interests, you are allowing him to reclaim the incredibly influential role that his own passions and gifts can have on his outlook on life and his vision of success.

In my office, I usually have students come up with personal goals after they learn about our different study and organizational techniques, but when working with your own child, talking about his personal interests can be a much more inviting way to start the conversation than focusing on their missing homework assignments, messy backpack, and poor grades. Sitting down to ask your son about his personal goals and aspirations can lead to the same changes in perspective that I witness in my office. It can start as a casual conversation in the car or as a topic brought up around the dinner table. Maybe he won't share a great deal with you right away, but just plant the seed, and chances are he'll take it from there and start to reframe his thought process and visualize his goals and desires. By taking this step, you are actively helping your son become more engaged and invested in his own personal success. *A word of caution:* This discussion cannot be out of the blue or prying in any way—a sudden show of interest from a previously detached parent will sink the conversation before it starts. So maybe it's a gradual process for you and your son, something that develops over several conversations.

Encourage your son to explore the answers to these three questions:

1. How would you choose to spend a free day?

2. If you could do anything with your life, what would it be and why?

3. What dream would you go after if you knew that you could not fail?

All too often we inadvertently focus on external rewards (getting an A on a test, making the honor roll, getting into a certain college) rather than looking at the internal factors that motivate each of us to feel that the possibilities are limitless. When your son is excited about something—anything—his whole countenance will change—and his outlook on life will improve. By asking your son what he is interested in accomplishing, you are inviting him to visualize the success that he may not be finding right now in his life. You are encouraging him to look beyond the narrow, short-term goals of turning in homework and acing quizzes, and allowing him to explore the bigger picture of his dreams and inspirations. You're also helping him

> By asking your son what he is interested in accomplishing, you are inviting him to visualize the success that he may not be finding right now in his life.

reframe his own way of thinking to see organization and study skills as stepping-stones or the means to an end, rather than an overwhelming burden.

His Dreams, His Goals

Even parents who thought they knew exactly what their son wanted or wished for are often surprised by the things they learn when they start a conversation around the three questions listed in the previous section. The truth is, your goals for your son may be very different from his own goals for himself. And once you remove yourself (and others—grandparents, siblings, well-meaning neighbors or teachers) from the framework and allow him to figure out his own goals, his behavior will begin to change without the nagging, fear, and annoyances that typically abound in parent–child relationships. Once your son has the freedom to establish and solidify his own passions and pursuits, the most appropriate role you can play as a parent is to help him cultivate those passions and convert them into goals. Let's say your son's answer to question 2 was simply, "Art." A good response to turn that into a short-term goal might be, "Is there some way you would want to get more involved with that? Summer art class, art class at school?" It's important not to judge the answers, so that your son feels comfortable communicating his true interests—the answers might surprise you!

When your son sets his own goals, he is accountable and responsible for his own destiny, and that is a very powerful elixir for a young man. Most adults aspire to have control of their own successful futures; for an adolescent or teenage boy to be given that same freedom of understanding and power to achieve can be pivotal to his personal growth and development. Even from as early as the fifth or sixth grade, this sense of responsibility is a powerful change agent. Instead of being coddled and directed, these boys are asked, "What do you want to do and how can we help you (and, most important, how can you help yourself) get there?"

It still astonishes me and makes me a little teary-eyed when the kids who were once completely and utterly disorganized walk in with binders, planners, and books in order; with a plan for their evening or week; and with everything pretty much in place. When Henry first came to my office the summer before his junior year, he had recently been diagnosed with attention deficit/hyperactivity disorder (ADHD). Charismatic and funny, Henry was the kid everyone in school knew as the class clown, and he genuinely liked to be liked. He played water polo and swam for his high school teams and practiced the drums nightly in his garage to release stress. Sitting across from me for the first time, he seemed to have a consistent beat going in his head, and his hands thrummed along the edge of the table like drumsticks.

Henry knew that his grades did not reflect his academic abilities, and I could see that his confidence in himself had begun to wane. He was the type of boy some teachers might mistakenly judge as unmotivated and lazy, but besides being easily distracted (a symptom of his ADHD), he wanted to do well in school and would really benefit from having an organizational system.

> Henry knew that his grades did not reflect his academic abilities, and I could see that his confidence in himself had begun to wane.

It took me almost a full semester to convince Henry to try to study without listening to music, and he loved to question me and clarify different aspects of his organizational and time-management plans. By the end of the semester, he admitted that he did, honestly, work more efficiently without music—he had just never tried it before and was resistant because he thought it would be boring. But he dialed back slowly—switching from lyrical to instrumental music and then deciding that no music was better for him than instrumental music.

At the end of our first session, I gave Henry a goals worksheet and explained to him that everyone in the office comes up with goals. He quickly became serious and focused. His eyes widened as he thought of the possibilities, and he started to think quietly and consciously. After a moment, he scribbled on the page: "Play the drums for an audience of more than fifty people."

"Sounds great," I said. "You can do it."

And he did. Less than a month later, he ran into my office beaming.

"Guess what, Ana? I made my goal." He was practically jumping up and down with anticipation.

"And," he continued, "my dad videotaped it and it's on YouTube. Want to check it out?"

We went to the computer, and Henry started to fill in everyone in the office on his school activities director's request that he play a drum solo in his high school's rally—an audience of at least fifteen hundred people, quite a bit more than the fifty people he'd put in his goal—and he'd accepted. With his friends' encouragement and his parents on board as well, he went for it. We watched as, despite his nerves, he performed in front of the crowd so confidently that when he dropped one of his drumsticks midway through the piece, he simply pretended that he'd planned it all along and kept right on playing. At the end of his performance, just as he had always dreamed of, the crowd went wild, and consequently Henry was asked to play at almost every rally thereafter.

In the next year and a half that he worked with us, Henry's successes mounted. He began to adapt the organizational and time-management strategies and became proactive in both his academic and extracurricular pursuits. His GPA improved from a 2.8 to a 3.5, and he even surprised his guidance counselor with strong SAT scores. He played the drums on a Bay Area morning FM radio show, reaching thousands of listeners. He became a leader among his peers and was asked to be a student retreat leader during his senior year. His confidence reached new heights, and he became the student he had always hoped he could be.

Achieving one of his personal goals was an important step for Henry on his path to reaching his academic ones. He needed to believe in himself and to develop his own inner self-confidence. He also needed others to validate and believe in his dreams. Even though he outwardly appeared to have a strong sense of self, playing in front of a huge audience of his peers gave him the confidence that he could meet and even exceed his own goals.

Three Academic and Three Personal Goals: Measurable and Specific

Talking about goals is the first step in helping your son believe in his own abilities and having him think about what he wants to accomplish. In general, my experience has been that boys really enjoy setting goals, and it's not difficult for them to come up with their lists of personal and academic ones. The process of setting goals motivates them to think about what they can achieve, and they get a tremendous sense of accomplishment as they start to reach each goal—which tends to motivate them to set the bar for themselves even higher.

Every semester, students who work in our office come up with three academic and three personal goals. We tend to focus on shorter-term goals that can be achieved in the next semester or over the next school year (which seems like an eternity to many teenagers). For academic goals, we suggest that students focus on habits they need to improve—such as writing in their planner every day or completing homework without distractions. Personal goals are whatever a student may choose—and it's really important to honor the individuality that each young person brings to determining what he personally wants to accomplish. Some of my favorites have been: "Get no detentions,"

"Get a part in the play," "Make the seventh grade volleyball team," "Play more golf with my dad," and "Pass my driver's license test the first time."

It's important to give boys free reign in this area and also to make sure the goals they write down are things they personally want to achieve, not goals they think others might have in mind for them. Many times, a goal that is seemingly simple to a parent—doing homework at the dining room table, for instance—is actually a monumental step in the eyes of a young man. I have also seen boys achieve goals that many adults probably thought to be overly ambitious, so I refrain from making commentary on the appropriateness of goals. Instead, I encourage boys to focus on goals that they feel that they can accomplish within the next semester or school year and help them figure out what steps they need to take to achieve those goals. Setting individual goals, outside of the academic framework of school, helps boys expand their vision to recognize that there is more to living an active and interesting life than merely focusing on getting good grades and doing well in school.

The following sections present some tips and suggestions to keep in mind about setting goals.

Make Goal-Setting a Family Affair

Each family has a different dynamic, and you probably know what works best in your family. Even parents who were skeptical are often surprised to see how their son's motivation increased once everyone in the family became seriously invested. Although no one is required to share his or her goals, it is helpful when family members publicly declare what they want to accomplish and spend even an hour thinking through how they are going to get there.

While you might not have academic goals, you can certainly set financial or health goals that are measured and specific and in line with your child's academic ones. One mom who did this with her son loved to bake. She could spend days happily baking away in the kitchen creating masterpieces. She seemed to really dislike her office job; I think her dreams of becoming a chef had somehow been thwarted in her earlier years. I suggested that she set goals with her son, who was in the eighth grade, to try to encourage him to follow through. That weekend, she and her son had a great conversation and each came up with a few goals for themselves. She set the goal to take a weekend baking class at the San Francisco Culinary Institute. So, while her son was trying to figure out how to master basic algebra, she found herself taking baby steps into a new career in the culinary arts.

Encourage Self-Competition

Famed ballet dancer Mikhail Baryshnikov once said, "I do not try to dance better than anyone else. I only try to dance better than myself." I love that quote, and I often use it with students to get them to concentrate their efforts on improving themselves rather than focusing on what everyone around them is doing. Most boys love competition, and will create mini-competitions out of just about anything (Who can run down the hall faster? Who can eat more cupcakes in a minute?). Encouraging them to compete—with themselves—will actually help them develop the intrinsic motivation that is crucial for creating a sense of personal values and passions. Especially while boys are growing and developing, they are all at different places at different times and need to learn to celebrate their personal progress rather than constantly compare themselves to their peers. By turning the competition inward, boys can focus on where they want to go and what they

By turning the competition inward, boys can focus on where they want to go and what they want to do, rather than constantly looking around to see if they measure up.

want to do, rather than constantly looking around to see if they measure up. Though competition seems natural, it is often a losing game—we can always find someone faster, smarter, more attractive, more successful. Reframe the thought process to focus on intrinsic or internal motivators: "Did you improve from where you were last week?" instead of "Did you get a better grade than Johnny on that test?"

Now, you might be reading this and thinking, "I mean, aren't college admissions, vying for jobs, financial success—aren't they all one big competition?" Or "After all, if you aren't better than the next guy, you're not going to get into the right school, which will lead to the right job and the right wife and the right life, right?" It's endless. But by focusing on self-improvement, these kids can carve their own niche for themselves where they are likely to be *more* successful than if they were constantly looking around and wasting energy thinking about whether they measured up. In doing so, they will also end up happier, better-adjusted individuals because they won't be judging their success or defining themselves by the success or missteps of others (neither of which they have any control over).

A couple of years ago, a high school junior named Dominic (a Creative Wonder) started working with me on his organizational and time-management skills. He had a wide variety of interests—basketball, swimming, hanging out with friends—but his main passion was filmmaking. On the weekends, he would get his friends together and direct movies for fun and usually got eight to twelve of his classmates involved in his highly orchestrated endeavors. For class projects, he would often go above and beyond to create elaborate and highly creative films that were truly awe-inspiring. On several occasions, teachers would ask to keep his work as an example of outstanding work for future classes. Instead of merely focusing on doing better than his classmates or getting an A, Dominic used his personal passion to promote his academic success and, in doing so, created his own playing field instead of relying on others to define success. Thanks to these efforts, he became a top student with a variety of different interests who was able to find success both in the classroom, with his projects, and outside of the classroom, with his other filmmaking accomplishments.

Write Down the Interim Steps and Time Frame

On the goals worksheet I use in my office, there is space beneath each goal for the student to think of the necessary steps to reach it (a sample worksheet can be found on pages 72–73). By writing down smaller steps and getting students to think incrementally, goals become less overwhelming and more achievable than if they're left as a single huge milestone looming in the distant future.

Recently, one of the high school sophomores I work with, Luke, listed as a personal goal that he wanted to climb Mount Whitney over the summer. While he was an active student with an engaging personality, we both knew that particular goal would be an incredible challenge. The hike was about twenty-two miles round trip with an elevation gain of over 6,100 feet, and he needed a permit from the Forest Service to attempt it. Luke had signed up for the adventure as a part of a group that takes teens on mountain-climbing expeditions as a way to help them learn how to overcome other obstacles in their lives. Needless to say, Luke knew that he'd have to get into shape before tackling the mountain, but when I noticed that several weeks had gone by without hearing

> By writing down smaller steps and getting students to think incrementally, goals become less overwhelming and more achievable than if they're left as a single huge milestone looming in the distant future.

him report on any incremental progress, we sat down to talk about it.

"What do you think you could do to get into condition to make the climb?" I asked him. He thought about it and I gave him some time to process and work out the steps.

"I could go to the Y and work out," he said.

"Great," I replied. "When can you go?"

He thought some more. "I can go Thursdays after school. I have guitar lessons on Monday, and have chess team practice on Tuesday and Wednesday right after school."

"Terrific. Is one day a week going to be enough?"

"I can run on Saturday mornings, too."

It was a good plan that didn't adversely affect anything else in his personal and academic schedule, so we wrote it down in his planner just like any other homework assignment. After a few weeks, we sat down to reassess; he added some weight training and later in the spring increased his exercise regimen to include hiking up a smaller mountain with a loaded backpack. By the summer, he was fit to climb Mount Whitney and did it just as he had envisioned. If he hadn't developed the incremental steps, he may still have been able to complete the climb but likely not with the confidence and strength he brought to it by setting and achieving interim goals.

Focus on Improving Organizational and Study Habits

For academic goals, focus on improving organizational and study habits, rather than on the grades themselves. In the upcoming chapters, I will talk about the different habits students have found effective in improving their organization and time-management skills. I strongly encourage students to focus on incorporating these habits into their goals (for example, studying two hours a night without distractions or completing test review sheets and making flash cards two nights ahead of time) instead of specific grade goals. Other good goals include keeping binders organized and writing down assignments daily in the planner. Over and over, I have seen that when a student focuses on the goals, the improvement in grades will come—and the improvement will often be even better than they once could have imagined.

Over and over, I have seen that when a student focuses on the goals, the improvement in grades will come—and the improvement will often be even better than they once could have imagined.

Take Scott, for example. When he first started coming to my office, he had a 2.6 GPA, had a backpack that was a black hole for papers, and carried around a binder that was missing a front cover. If he had set a GPA goal for himself when he first came in, his goal would have been a 3.0. But once he started studying, becoming better organized, and finding success, the upward mobility caused him to continue to improve, eventually ending up with a 3.3 GPA—higher than he originally thought possible. We talked about his dramatic improvement, and he reflected that if he had made a specific grade goal when he walked in, he probably would have become comfortable with a smaller gain and would have stopped pushing himself and looking for ways to continue to make progress. By focusing on the study habits instead of the grade, he attained a level of personal improvement he once thought impossible.

Keep the List of Goals Visible and Handy

Encourage your child to keep the list of goals in a place where he will see it regularly. More than a few of my students put their goals on the bulletin board in their room where they have a gentle daily reminder of what they would like to accomplish. Other students have their goals sheet at the front of one of their binders, or stapled to the first page of their planner. If you are heading toward making the goals a family affair, I would even encourage you to put your goals in a place where you can all see them—on the refrigerator door, perhaps, or right near your family's catch-all area.

Check In and Reassess Regularly

Checking in should be a positive reflection rather than a condemnation of what is or is not happening. It is a way to reflect, even in just five or ten minutes once every week, on what is working and what is still a struggle. It's all a process; over time, the habits can be adapted as a part of an overall framework of defining and finding personal success. Especially with younger middle schoolers, having regular check-ins are vital to maintaining consistency.

> Especially with younger middle schoolers, having regular check-ins are vital to maintaining consistency.

I recommend choosing a specific time, rather than having a random check-in moment potentially inserted between band practice and dinner at Grandma's, but every family dynamic is different and schedules don't always allow for a set time. For some families, Sunday evenings can be an easy time to do a regular check-in.

Most of the goals students set are usually of a shorter term—semester or school-year-long goals. For preteens and teenagers, life, interests, and passions tend to shift, particularly when students reflect on what they are interested in accomplishing and pursuing; we should encourage that reflection and reassessment as part of their personal growth process. In addition, they may achieve a goal in a short time and then want to set another goal, so reassessing goals on a regular basis is important. Making five-year plans with a twenty-five-year-old might make sense, but with a twelve- or fifteen-year-old, a lot can change as different opportunities and interests develop. I encourage most students to reassess their goals at the beginning of each new semester, as well as at the beginning of summer vacation.

Track Progress

One of the phrases most often heard in my office is "in my entire life," as in, "That was the hardest test in my entire life!" Or, "I've never been so embarrassed in my entire life!" Teenagers tend to live in the moment and often find it difficult to think back to even the very recent past and remember where they started and how far they've come. Keeping old goals sheets is a great way to show them evidence of their progress. It's always encouraging for me to flip to an old completed goal sheet when a student is having a bad day or is frustrated by a setback. It's a surefire way to help him regain some confidence.

> It's always encouraging for me to flip to an old completed goal sheet when a student is having a bad day or is frustrated by a setback. It's a surefire way to help him regain some confidence.

Lars was one of the first students I worked with when I was starting out as a chemistry tutor. He had a bit of a Seemingly Satisfied Slacker in him, was flunking chemistry, and spent most of the class sitting in the back cracking jokes with his friends. Even the teacher had given up on him. Lars, however, needed to raise his GPA to be eligible to play on the baseball team in the spring, and raising his F in chemistry was the best place to start.

We began working together in October, and Lars almost immediately made progress. He started reading the textbook and thoroughly completing the homework, which meant that he found himself understanding the material and getting As on his tests. But, because he tended to live in the present, Lars quickly forgot that he had been flunking the class merely six weeks earlier and actually began getting angry whenever he missed a single point on a test.

"Look at this," he told me a few weeks in. "I got a nineteen out of twenty."

"Fantastic," I said.

But he just frowned. "How did I miss that? That's stupid!"

We went over the test and figured out that his one-point error was an easy one to make and didn't reflect his hard work and knowledge. Even though I knew it was unlikely that Lars would ever resort to being the class clown sitting in the back of the room again, I opened his binder and flipped to his very first goals sheet. Under academic goals, the first one listed was "Pass chemistry."

"That was only a month and a half ago," I reminded him. "Look how far you've come in such a short time."

On days when nothing seems to be going their way, teenagers can get a confidence boost by having a little history to put things in perspective.

Why Setting Goals Is My Favorite Part of My Work

I always learn a lot about students by looking at their goals. By writing down goals, students are saying, "I think I can do this, and I want to do this." Many boys still have that childhood sense of fearlessness at their core and are actually willing to take risks and push themselves. I can't tell you the number of times I've seen boys come into my office slouching, sullen, and frustrated—and then transformed when they pick up that pen to challenge themselves by setting their goals. It's as if this were the first time someone had asked them, "What do you want to do?" and, more important, "How are you going to get there?" That initial look of eagerness and anticipation is topped only by the excitement in their eyes when they reach a goal they've set for themselves, a goal that once seemed far off in the distance. For preteens, giving them the ability to think about what they want to achieve—and start contemplating ways to achieve the results they desire—is a powerful motivator.

The other great by-product of boys achieving their goals is the effect it has on everyone around them, particularly their families. The parents who initially dragged their son in to see me often take as much pride in their son's triumphs in meeting personal goals as the boy does himself. And let's not forget the teachers, administrators, and counselors who watch with (often dumbfounded) admiration when he accomplishes something that he has put his mind to—the ripple effects are endless.

Summary

One great way to help your son focus on personal growth and satisfaction rather than just academic results is to work with him to set specific goals. It's an integral part of what I do in my office, and it's one of the most rewarding things you can do with your teen. Use the worksheet on pages 72–73 to help your son set three personal and three academic goals, and when you do it, remember the following:

- These are *his* goals, not yours or anyone else's, and if you let him choose (within reason), he's much more likely to take responsibility for meeting those goals.

- After he sets his goals, make sure that he is able to follow up. Schedule check-ins and progress reports. He can even reassess the goals if necessary.

- For academic goals, focus on study habits and skills, rather than GPA. If the right goals are set and met, the grades will follow.

◼ ACADEMIC AND PERSONAL GOALS WORKSHEET

What do you want to achieve? Think about goals that you want to accomplish—reflect, dream, and aspire. Want to make the basketball team? Do well in school? Set specific goals and believe in yourself—make it happen!

Academic Goals

1. _____

What I need to do to achieve this goal:

_____

_____

_____

2. _____

What I need to do to achieve this goal:

_____

_____

_____

3. _____

What I need to do to achieve this goal:

_____

_____

_____

Personal Goals

1. _____

What I need to do to achieve this goal:

_____

_____

_____

2. _____

What I need to do to achieve this goal:

_____

_____

_____

3. _____

What I need to do to achieve this goal:

_____

_____

_____

5

Binders, Planners, and Other Essential Tools

Let's face it—most kids would rather get their wisdom teeth extracted, sans anesthesia, than organize their binders and backpack with their parents (and probably vice versa). But the key to academic success lies with these tools and how they're used. Unfortunately, I often see students whose well-intentioned parents buy either the wrong supplies or just too many of them. I always have at least one kid every semester with a top-of-the-line $150 graphing calculator when all he needs is a $17 scientific calculator, or $10 fully padded binders that take up too much space instead of the utilitarian hardback binders that can be found for $5 or less. As a result, these students actually start off at a *disadvantage*—overwhelmed by gear that often just gets in the way.

But of course not all tools are physical ones. When I originally started working with students, I was surprised at the number who, although they appeared completely disorganized, had some sort of complicated system they'd developed and stuck with, even though it was failing them miserably. They knew they needed *something* to keep

They knew they needed *something* to keep them on track, but because they had never learned an effective strategy, they were sticking with the best one they had, even if all it delivered was disappointment and even, sadly, *added* stress to their lives.

them on track, but because they had never learned an effective strategy, they were sticking with the best one they had, even if all it delivered was disappointment and even, sadly, *added* stress to their lives.

Getting the right tools to be organized does not need to be expensive, nor does it need to be stressful. One of the most important reasons my work teaching organization and time management to preteen and teenage boys is effective is that it's simple—the young person walks away thinking, "Hey, this is easy . . . I can *totally* do this."

The Elusive and All-Important Key: An Organized Binder

The single most important organizational tool your son will need is an effective, organized binder, preferably one for each subject. Some other organizational experts sing the praises of accordion files—in my experience, however, accordion file folders can be one of the worst things ever created for a teenage boy. They create a black hole of papers, which inevitably end up stuffed into the wrong section and are as good as lost.

Miles was the first student I ever worked with. He was flunking chemistry, and his guidance counselor asked if I'd be willing to work with him, as he needed to pass chemistry in order to graduate. Miles was a true Scattered Charmer—a friendly and fun kid. His family lived near the beach in Santa Cruz, and he commuted about an hour each way to school every day. The first time we met, he brought no backpack and instead was holding just one plastic accordion file folder with dog-eared papers protruding from the sides. After chatting for a few minutes, I discovered that he had failed to turn in multiple assignments, had misplaced others, and his grade was a dismal 30 percent—below an F. Not understanding chemistry was clearly only part of Miles's problem.

"You know, I think you might find more success with a binder," I said.

"But this accordion file is great!" Miles replied. "I have everything for class right here."

"How's that working for you?" I asked, gently reminding him why we were meeting *twice* a week.

Within fifteen minutes, we started going through the accordion folder and finding long-lost assignments (some that were never turned in, even though they had been completed), triple copies of worksheets (because he thought he had lost the first two), and the course syllabus. We separated everything into four different sections—notes, homework, handouts, and tests/quizzes—and put the papers into a three-ring binder, the first step in helping Miles develop an effective and efficient organizational system for himself. Within eight weeks, Miles made up assignments—his teacher generously allowed him to turn in late work with minimal penalty—turned in homework, studied for quizzes, and went from a 30 percent to a 72 percent, more than doubling his percentage and enabling him to graduate.

It's not that Miles was defiant about changing his ways; he had just never, in all his years of schooling, been presented with another method of organization. At the end of our

> It's not that Miles was defiant about changing his ways; he had just never, in all his years of schooling, been presented with another method of organization.

ten weeks working together, he was able to find papers more quickly, and everything had a place within his system, making him more confident that he had ownership over the process.

Binder Basics

Here are the details of how your son's binders should be organized. Though I strongly suggest that students use a separate three-ring binder for each subject, with five tabbed dividers, I realize that is not always possible. Separate subject binders dramatically reduce *co-mingling*: when papers from one subject end up with papers from another subject, inevitably resulting in a frenzied last-minute search. Every parent can recall a fateful evening when some important English worksheet ended up in the math section and a half an hour was spent frantically going through the backpack, tearing apart the desk and closet with, depending on the age of the student, a diverting accompaniment of tears, tantrum, and/or tirade.

A simple, hardback binder costs between $3 and $5 at most office supply stores (and cheaper at discount warehouses). It doesn't need to be anything fancy. For most classes, a one-inch binder is sufficient, though smaller ones might be used for classes that don't typically require a lot of written work, like art or chorus. Some math or history classes have a lot of papers and handouts, and for those classes I recommend a one-and-a-half-inch binder. Keep in mind—and I will discuss this later in the chapter—that your child should not be carrying a year's worth of school papers on his back. At the end of every grading period, he can create a file system in your home and file everything away. So in most cases, a one-inch binder for each class is sufficient.

If your son's teachers have a method of organizing dividers that they require for their students, then your time organizing should be spent helping your child create the system required. If, however, the teacher has no set strategy for organization, this is the method that my students have found especially helpful. Everything should be hole-punched, with no papers left in the front of the binder or elsewhere. In the very front of the first divider, he

> Everything should be hole-punched, with no papers left in the front of the binder or elsewhere.

should place his syllabus or green sheet for the class. Using five tab dividers, papers should be separated and sorted into the following sections: notes, homework, handouts, tests/quizzes, and paper.

NOTES

The notes section is, of course, for any notes taken in class. Every day, ideally, a student should take a piece of paper out of the paper section, put the date on top, and take notes on it from that day of class. If there is space left over (say the teacher gave only a half of a page of notes that day) he can continue using that page the next day in class by just putting the new date midway down the page. Writing the date on the notes helps him recognize that the notes taken back in September—while possibly containing crucial information for the midterm or final exam—are not as relevant for a quiz in late November on more recent material.

TIP: I strongly discourage using spiral notebooks if at all possible. Inevitably, your child will forget/lose/discard the spiral notebook, and his notes will be out of order. If he uses binder paper, he can easily get back on track even if he forgets the binder one day. Also, carrying around spiral notebooks adds considerable weight (and don't get me started on the child who thinks that he should have one spiral notebook for five classes. That is co-mingling at its worst!).

HOMEWORK

The homework section of a binder is the key to reclaiming the sanity of both parents and students. If the homework is a worksheet or other similar assignment, the student places it at the front of this section.

He then knows where it is later that afternoon or evening when he goes to do his homework, and it eliminates the lost-worksheet scenario in which you are calling another parent (or your son is texting his friend from class) to beg for the questions from the misplaced worksheet. Once the homework is completed, it goes back into the homework section, and then, *and only then*, can it be checked off on the planner (I talk about the planner in a minute). If it's not back in the binder, it's not done and cannot be checked off in the planner. This system is simple and eliminates the "I did the assignment but I left it on my printer" scenario.

> If it's not back in the binder, it's not done and cannot be checked off in the planner.

HANDOUTS

One section in the binder is for handouts given by the teacher, and what goes in here depends on the class. For an English class, short stories could go here. For a science class, lab reports or other worksheets might go here. Realistically, there are many things that could go in either Notes or in Handouts, and it's up to the student to determine what works best for him. Whenever I am going through papers with a student, I always let the student decide, because after all, it is his system, and it gives him more ownership of the process. The fact that he can make the decision makes him feel more in control, and inevitably—as long as he is consistent in grouping things together—he will know where things are and be able to find everything.

TESTS/QUIZZES

I encourage students to keep all the tests and quizzes (especially the ones with scores that were lower than ideal). Sometimes, a student gets a lower quiz score than expected, and in frustration he stuffs the (unfair and stupid!) quiz in the bottom of his backpack, only to be found months later in fragments—useful to no one. Again, it's all about the presentation. Explain that the quizzes are usually the basis for the tests and the tests are usually the basis for final exams; by hanging on to all of them your son can actually save time and make life easier (a win–win). In my experience, students are typically won over.

> Explain that the quizzes are usually the basis for the tests and the tests are usually the basis for final exams; by hanging on to all of them your son can actually save time and make life easier (a win–win).

One cautionary tale here. When Gus, the Seemingly Satisfied Underachiever, was a high school junior, he hid a few of his quizzes in random places because he did not want his mom to find out that he was doing poorly on his physics quizzes (because she would stress out, he confided, and he didn't want to have to deal with her stress). He was certain he would do well on the upcoming test and that his grade wouldn't be permanently affected by a few low quiz scores. If you really want your kid to learn from his mistakes, you need to be okay with quizzes that are sometimes less than ideal.

PAPER

Reinforced binder paper is one of the best things ever invented, simply because it reduces the problem of paper tearing at the holes. The back of each binder should have twenty to thirty sheets of this paper, enough to last a few weeks without being an overwhelming burden on your son's back. Time and time again I encounter the student who puts two hundred sheets of binder paper in *each* binder and wonders why his backpack is so incredibly heavy.

Creating Organized Binders

When students come into my office to get organized, we go through every single piece of paper, errant marker, and pencil case to help them get a fresh start. The work generally goes quite quickly and efficiently; after all, I've been doing this for years, and I've seen most boys' situations numerous times. My office is a place where students know they are coming to get organized. It's a straightforward place with a straightforward objective.

So I'll be the first to acknowledge what happens in my office is not an exact mirror of what you'll be setting up at home. For instance, because I don't share your particular parent–child dynamic, I have the luxury of my words being more likely to be heard as helpful advice as opposed to a parent's seemingly nagging advice. Sadly, this is true even if my words are the verbatim transcript of what you say at home. Such is the nature of many parent–son relationships.

Furthermore, I don't personally know your child, so you may already be reading this and saying to yourself, "Does she really expect [insert son's name here] to be happily spending his Sunday afternoon at the dining room table organizing his papers, and with *me* sitting next to him? And better yet, why would I want to put *myself* through that?"

My only answer to this is experience. I've seen it happen successfully, again and again, and often with parents who simply couldn't imagine it when we got started. I readily admit that it doesn't work all the time, but it does more often than most parents would think.

So it shouldn't surprise you that the key to starting this process is to have a strategy in place, and there are some fairly simple things to keep in mind when you set out.

Schedule a Time

Nobody likes to be blindsided, least of all a preteen or teenage boy. Schedule a time in advance that you both commit to, with the attitude that this will help him spend less time looking for papers, completing homework, and getting stressed and will ultimately give him more time to do what he wants. Ask your son what time *he* thinks would work first, and in doing so, you let him feel like he has some power in the situation. From his response, find a time that works for both of you—say, Saturday afternoon at 3:00. Once you get started, it takes far less time than you ever imagined. I can usually get seven binders and a thousand papers organized in a little under two hours working midway through the semester with a thoroughly disorganized kid. It can either take you a little less time, if you are starting out earlier in the semester, or a little more time, if you start three weeks before the end of the grading period. The earlier, the better, obviously, but it's never too late.

Organize Yourself First or At the Same Time

A little organization never hurt anyone, and it might be worthwhile to set a good example. Perhaps one weekend you get your files in order, or ask your son to help you organize your closet (children, like the rest of us, are often more excited about helping someone else get organized than about organizing themselves). However, if working together doesn't work for the two of you, maybe working side by side will. Take opposite sides of the dining room or kitchen table, and then while he is cleaning out his backpack, you can work on organizing your own piles of paper or creating all those hanging file folders you have been meaning to do for ages.

> However, if working together doesn't work for the two of you, maybe working side by side will.

While doing so, you might be able to ask your son if there is anything in his room or elsewhere that he would like help organizing. Again, by asking you are giving him the opportunity to have power over his organizational efforts.

Use a Carrot

I have yet to meet a child who truly *wants* to be more stressed and secretly desires to spend *more* time on his homework only to receive lower grades. For him to then get hit with the refrain, "I really think you need to get organized because you are getting terrible grades" is not a winning presentation. Inherently, we all want to feel good about ourselves and feel that we have the power to succeed at something, somewhere.

So reframe the argument to focus on the positive benefits rather than the negative consequences. First, point out what good attributes he already has; fish to find something by asking him what he thinks his strengths are. Then, tell him that you want to support him to enhance those positive qualities. Present this idea of organization to your son as a way to spend less time on his homework, get better grades, feel more in control, and ultimately have more time to do what he enjoys doing (shooting hoops, hanging out with friends, painting, whatever). Ultimately, I am not a fan of hours and hours of homework, but I think it's important for your son to know what he needs to do to get where he wants to go. Once he sees that strategy, he will develop the motivation and drive to reach heights he may have previously thought unattainable.

Pass No Judgments, but Leave No Paper Unturned

When you sit down with your child and go through his papers, avoid the commentary and look at the ultimate goal of helping him get a fresh, clean start. No need to belabor the point that his papers are out of order (clearly, or you wouldn't be spending such a lovely Saturday afternoon sorting through crumpled papers). The ancient Chinese philosopher Lao-Tzu famously writes, "The journey of a thousand miles began with a single step." With that in mind, every piece of paper that finds a home or the recycling bin, whether crumpled or otherwise, is another step closer to being organized. Resist the impulse to criticize, and if your son begins to criticize himself, refocus him on the positive changes he's starting to make.

When All Else Fails, Outsource

Giving your son the proper tools to be successful does not mean that you necessarily have to sit there and organize all the papers and create neat binders, especially if you think that it would shorten either one of your life spans. I am realistic here; there are some parents and sons for whom going through papers is just not a good idea for either party. Perhaps there is a college student or organized older cousin who could be enlisted in this effort. One of my former students, Mary, helped her younger brother get organized by helping him label all his dividers and separate all his binders before he started his freshman year of high school. It was simple for her to do, and he responded well to having her help him versus working with his mom. As a parent, you probably know to whom he will respond best; try enlisting that person's support in getting the nuts and bolts of the organization done.

FAQ: BINDERS

1. My son refuses to take notes in class and says that the teacher doesn't say anything that he needs to write down for notes, but

when I talk to the teacher, she says that my son sits there listlessly in class.

Here is how I describe taking notes in class to my students: Most teachers, when they lecture, are giving you all the material they want you to learn for upcoming tests and quizzes. Essentially, they are giving you the answers to the test! *Here they are, just write them down, here is what I want you to know!* Again, it's all in the presentation. If you present taking notes as something that will ultimately make his life easier, helping him get what he wants, he is more likely to become motivated.

Now, this assumes that your son can easily take notes and does not struggle with issues surrounding note taking. Sometimes students tell me that they really don't know what to write down, and I suggest that they start with what the teacher has scribbled on the board, and then add any other interesting facts around that. Taking good notes comes with practice, and everyone needs to start somewhere. *Caveat:* If your child has a diagnosed learning difficulty (see Chapter 10) for which taking notes while listening decreases his ability to retain information, have him proactively work with the teacher to see if he can get a copy of notes *ahead* of a class lecture if at all possible. That way he can spend most of his time listening and simply adding a note or two as he listens.

If a student is really challenged by note taking, I also suggest he compare his notes with those of a friend, so that both students can see what they missed or what else would be helpful. Plus he can always go right to the source—most teachers will be happy to glance over a student's notes and perhaps even fill in blanks or tell him where he strayed from the important points.

2. What about having one overall homework folder where all assignments that need to be turned in that day are kept, regardless of what class they're for?

Sometimes parents or teachers recommend this method. Typically, it's better to put everything back in the homework section of each binder. If the homework folder gets lost, for example, so does every assignment for every class that is due that day—that would make for a very rough Monday morning.

3. My son's teacher has her own method for organizing a binder. She inspects binders and then gives a grade on it.

In my experience, about 80 percent of teachers leave it to their students to create an organizational system, but that leaves the other 20 percent. By all means use the teacher's method if this is the case. The exact organization method of the binder isn't crucial, as long as you and your son can keep the essentials straight (no co-mingling, if possible, etc.).

4. My son insists that chorus does not need a binder. What do you think?

I always have boys who tell me that classes like chorus or art or health don't need binders, because they don't "have anything in that class." But then, as we are going through their binders and backpacks, we find sheet music for the "Maple Leaf Rag," art handouts on the Renaissance, or a health packet stuffed into the back of another binder. So, yes, chorus needs a binder—maybe a half-inch binder if there really aren't a lot of papers, but the syllabus and sheet music need to go somewhere other than the back of the math binder.

5. That is a lot of binders—my son has seven classes—how can he manage it all?

I work with a lot of students who have seven classes—though many schools have block scheduling, in which students have only a few classes on each day. If that is the case, your son needs to have only the three or four binders for that day's classes in his backpack. If he has a schedule in which he has all classes every day, then I would suggest he use his locker between classes to store books and binders that he doesn't need—some kids really refuse to use their locker, but adopting that little habit cuts down on how much weight students have to carry on their back.

6. My son is in junior high, does not have a locker, and one day a week he has all of his classes. He cannot carry around seven binders. What should we do?

I completely sympathize with this problem, which most of the junior high students I know have. A few options: (1) You could get him a bigger backpack or a rolling backpack if he does not already have one. (2) If you really want to consolidate classes into one binder, look to consolidate electives or classes with the least amount of paperwork first: art and health for instance, or chorus and foods class. For those classes, put two sets of four dividers—one set for each class (notes, homework, handouts, test/quizzes)—with some paper in the back.

Organizing Binders After the Grading Period Is Complete

After the quarter, semester, or grading period is over, set aside an hour or two to refresh the binders. Get a box of manila file folders, have your son label one for each class (for example, "Biology: Semester 1") and have him clean out his binder and file the material he thinks he should keep. If the end-of-the-school-year final is cumulative, make sure he keeps all the old tests and the midterm exam (if the teacher gives it back). He should be sure to keep quizzes, tests, or English papers that might be necessary at the end of the school year; this way he still knows where everything is and can access it easily, but does not have to carry it in his backpack and can start the new semester with a fresh start.

If the end-of-the-school-year final is cumulative, make sure he keeps all the old tests and the midterm exam (if the teacher gives it back).

Find a space for all the manila folders, either by providing a portable file box, a rolling file cart, or a space for his papers in your own filing cabinet if you have one.

The Other Essential: Planners

Many schools these days give out daily planners to their students, and the majority of these go underused and stuffed in the bottom of back-packs. School planners are often helpful because they list the different school schedule days or closures, but sometimes the space to list homework is so small that your child would have to be a magician to find enough room.

My favorite school planners are the ones that have the schedule for each day written out, and also give individual spaces for each class. So, if your student has class for periods 1, 3, and 5 on Tuesday, the school calendar lists those three blocks with individual spaces after each class title to write homework assignments. In case you or anyone you know is on the school planner purchasing committee (if such a thing exists), school planners that are organized in this way are excellent because each class has its own space for the student to fill in the assignments, and if a block is left empty the student knows he hasn't recorded his homework for that class.

If your child's school doesn't offer a planner, or if the planner is woefully inadequate for your son's needs, there are plenty of great ones out there—any office supply store typically has a few good options. Stick to planners with a full page for each day, so that there is plenty of space to write things down. *Note:* I have my students list their class rotation in their planner (for each day) at the start of each week—for instance, your son might write in English, math, and science on Monday and wood shop, band, and French on Tuesday—that makes them more aware and conscious about their upcoming week and what subjects they have on each day.

Also, encourage your son to maintain his own personal schedule in the planner. If he has soccer practice on Tuesdays and Thursdays at 4:00 and piano lessons on Monday at 5:00, those regular appointments should all be in his planner. No matter if he is in the sixth grade or a senior in high school, allowing him to know and think about his own activities and practices early is going to help him when you are no longer with him in college and beyond.

> If he has soccer practice on Tuesdays and Thursdays at 4:00 and piano lessons on Monday at 5:00, those regular appointments should all be in his planner.

TIP: Keeping in mind the suggestions about what features can make a planner more useful, have your child choose the planner that he wants to use (if you are purchasing a planner from an office supply store). It shouldn't just be presented to him, or it won't truly be "his."

FAQ: PLANNERS

1. My son's school has all the homework available online—does he still really need a planner?
Yes, absolutely! Regardless of whether homework is available online, students should be *writing down all their assignments in one place* so they (1) have control over their resources (woe to the kid who relies on the Internet when the connection goes down!) and (2) can create their own plan for getting the work done amid all their other activities (see "Online Homework," later in this chapter).

If your son is resistant to using the planner, again, *think presentation*. If he has all his assignments in one place, he will spend less time every evening calling friends, checking the online homework database (which can be wrong at times or the server could be down) and locating assignments from each individual binder. He can get right to work, which will help him finish his homework faster, resulting in more time to do whatever he pleases.

The Wired Challenge:
PDAs and Online Homework

Technology can be a great help in keeping boys on track, but I prefer to think of it primarily as a backup system for the binders and planners I already discussed. Two technologies in particular, PDAs (personal digital assistants, like iPhones and BlackBerrys) and online homework, can be great for this purpose. Unfortunately, they often get in the way and do more harm than good.

PDAs

Every now and then I have a student who insists on using a PDA device to track his homework assignments. This student is typically a Tech Master who thinks that every human endeavor should be done online. These kids insist that using the latest gadgets will keep them up-to-date and take up less space. Though I personally use a PDA to keep track of my appointments and other activities, I have never seen a junior high or high school student effectively keep track of homework and other activities in a PDA like an iPhone or BlackBerry, and for one main reason: *distractions*. Some PDAs have phone access, contacts, web access, music options, text messaging, games, and a camera. Can't you just hear your son saying he is checking his homework when he is really spending thirty quality minutes

> If your child has a PDA and likes to use it, he should *still use a written planner* to track his homework, long-term assignments, and tests and quizzes.

figuring out how to take impressive photos of his hand to forward to his friends?

Also, with PDAs, tracking long-term assignments can be cumbersome. Students often end up having a to-do list a mile long that becomes so annoying that they start to ignore it. If your child has a PDA and likes to use it, he should *still use a written planner* to track his homework, long-term assignments, and tests and quizzes.

Online Homework

Many schools now have all class assignments posted online using resources such as Edline or PowerSchool. This system is great as a backup if a student misses class and wants to find out the page number for the math assignment when all of his classmates are at practice. However, online homework has a negative side. Many students don't bother to open up their planners to write down the assignments in class because they figure they can go online later and just look it up. This plan often fails, of course. Teachers are human too, and they sometimes change an assignment in class and don't remember to update the website. Teachers can also forget to put an assignment (due Monday) on the website until late Sunday evening—after all, they told the class about it the previous week—or the school server was down. You get the drift.

A teacher who has been teaching history for more than thirty years at one of the high schools near my office is a legend, and everyone knows him—he even taught some of his current students' parents. But he refuses to use the computer, hates email, and thinks the school's online homework site is too cumbersome and a waste of his time. For a while, he did try to post the class assignments, but one out of every three entries was incorrect. Other times, he would change the dates of the test and then not update the computer system, so students would show up on Tuesday thinking the test was on Thursday and well, there went that test.

I encourage students to use the online system as a guide and re-source, but ultimately, *everything should be written down in the planner based on what a teacher says in class.* That approach is less stressful for the students because they have all their assignments in one place and can use the planner to develop their overall plan of attack.

Summary

Every job needs the right tools, and for academic organization and time management there really are two big ones: the binder and the planner. Although your child's school may have some guidelines in place for these tools, most don't. Here are my recommendations for getting started.

To Get Started
- Schedule a time to go through all his existing materials and make it as palatable as possible for everyone. You can help, do your own project, or find someone else to help your child.

For the Binder Itself
- Nothing fancy or expensive—it's really just about how it's organized.

- Five tabs: notes, homework, handouts, tests/quizzes, and paper

- No pockets; get a three-hole punch for handouts, tests, and review sheets; put looseleaf paper in tab 5.

- Remember, nothing is done until it's filed in the binder.

Planners
- If your child's school doesn't offer a custom planner, by all means have your child get one and encourage him to put every-thing in there, academic and social. Even if the school has

assignments online, he should copy everything into the planner. Online resources can be helpful but aren't as reliable as a hard-copy planner.

A HELPFUL SUPPLY LIST

Before you go to the office supply or discount supply store, consult the following list of essential supplies and then the short list of helpful but optional items. You may have many of these items around your home, so getting organized does not need to be costly.

Essentials

- Binders: 1 inch for most subjects, ½ inch for smaller subjects, 1½ inch for subjects that have a lot of papers

- Set of five tab dividers: one set for each binder

- Page-a-day planner: necessary if the school does not provide one or if the school-issued planner does not have enough room to list homework

- Reinforcements: for binder paper

- Reinforced binder paper

- Three-hole punch: a desk-size one for the house and a portable one for your son's backpack or binder

- Pencil pouch: made from canvas (the plastic ones can break or crack under pressure)

- Calculator: see what type your son needs for class (scientific or graphing); I like the Texas Instruments model because it's easy to use

- Stapler, tape, scissors: for the study space at home

- Markers, pencils, pens

- Big erasers: buy a couple

- Manila folders: for the post-semester storage

Optional

- Graph paper

- File box

- Book of quotations

- Non-electronic dictionary and thesaurus

6

Creating Space for Success

A Place to Study

When I first meet a student, I always ask him where he does his homework. Most respond, with pride, "My room." I then casually press a little further and ask what distractions they have in their room. The easy targets tell me they have a television, computer, and/or video game console—typical and obvious distractions for most boys. Others insist there are no distractions at all—until they see my knowing look and I remind them of their music and phone and text messaging. They soon realize that I am in on the secret—for most students, the bedroom is one of the *least effective* places to get things done.

Clay was frustrated that he was flunking the daily quizzes his English teacher was giving the class to make sure they were keeping up with the reading. He insisted that he *was* reading the book— Thomas Hardy's *Mayor of Casterbridge*—and thought he understood it as he was reading it, so I asked him where and when he was reading the book.

"I like to do all my reading right before I go to sleep," he replied earnestly, "while I'm lying in bed."

I am sure he learned that technique watching his parents, who are voracious readers and likely read books before turning in for the evening. However, his parents were likely reading those books for pleasure and probably didn't have reading quizzes on the material the next day.

I explained to Clay that because his brain associated his bed with sleep and rest, by lying down in his bed, he's in fact encouraging his body and mind to wind down for the day. Reading in bed at the end of the evening was *not* the most effective place for him to try and accomplish schoolwork.

"But it's so much more relaxing," he insisted.

I nodded knowingly. "How relaxing is it getting those quizzes back?" I asked.

Beware of the Bedroom

Clay's example is a fairly obvious one, but there are many other problems with working in a bedroom besides the tendency to fall prey to sleep, and not just for boys. Most adults do not find it effective to do their office work in their bedroom. Adults who work at home generally have a home office whenever possible or a space dedicated to their work. Many time-management and stress experts insist that individuals try to keep work—especially stressful work—out of the bedroom, which should be a place of rest and relaxation.

In the ancient Chinese art of feng shui, one of the most important principles is that a bedroom is a place for

Many time-management and stress experts insist that individuals try to keep work—especially stressful work—out of the bedroom, which should be a place of rest and relaxation.

rest and rejuvenation and that work should always be kept separate. Chi, or life force, flows through all objects in a space, and each item present in a room has some effect on whether chi moves freely or gets clogged up. A study area is place of work and inevitable stress—no student is ever completely unstressed—and this works against that need for relaxation. Alternatively, as with Clay, the converse can happen—the bed becomes a place that saps motivation and triggers a sleep response.

Senior feng shui practitioner Deborah Gee frequently consults with parents on how to create bedrooms and study spaces that are most intellectually and spiritually effective for children. She agrees that it is better for high school students to study in a separate space outside the bedroom if at all possible so that the bedroom can be a place of rest and sleep. Even having a study desk in the bedroom can make the mind active, and as children grow older, the bedroom should instead be a place of stillness and rest. Gee also suggests that a healthy live green plant be placed in the study area of the bedroom to promote clear thinking, and encourages parents to select the "knowledge center" of the house as the best study area. From a feng shui perspective, an ideal study space would be a quiet area free from distractions with medium light (if too harsh, the light can hinder focus), in the knowledge center of the house, and filled with tangible physical objects associated with learning and inspiration such as books, reference materials, and study aids.

Still, when I tell parents that one of *the most essential* starting points in this process is for their son to begin studying somewhere—*anywhere*—other than his bedroom, I often get resistance. In many cases, I sense that having the child complete homework in his room is the most convenient for the family dynamics of the home—the television is on elsewhere, a parent or grandparent is cooking dinner in the kitchen, or younger siblings are running around. Parents tell me that their son's desk is already set up in his room, and that his bedroom is the only space in the house where he can get away from the distractions.

At this point I remind them of when their son was very young. What did they think when he was off by himself and had been quiet, too quiet, for too long? That's right—that something must be wrong; he was probably up to no good or getting into something. For most preteen and teenage boys who struggle with organization and time management, being quiet in their room when they are supposed to be doing homework often means they are doing anything and everything but their homework.

> The average preteen or teenager, although fully intending to do homework, can distract himself for a full fifteen minutes (or more) simply by staring at the wall and daydreaming.

The average preteen or teenager, although fully intending to do homework, can distract himself for a full fifteen minutes (or more) simply by staring at the wall and daydreaming. One young man I interviewed admitted he was an expert at creating animals out of paperclips—and would keep them all in the side drawer of his desk—so that whenever his parents would walk in, he would quickly shut the drawer as if he was working diligently.

Even with a desk dedicated to homework (but generally covered with the assorted detritus of their daily lives), often these boys find themselves sitting on their bed, which of course reminds them of sleep (see Chapter 9). Combine lying on a bed with reading less-than-scintillating required school reading, and it's definitely a temptation for the mind to wander off into daydreams or even *real* dreams.

But as many of you know, the teenage boy's mind is susceptible to more distractions than just a comfy bed. When Damian first walked into my office, his mother walked in right behind him about to strangle him or cry, I'm not sure which. They'd just come from a conference with his history teacher, and Damian was flunking the class after forgetting to turn in the research paper due the previous week. I began by talking to him about his home life, particularly about how and where he did his homework. His mom interjected, explaining that even though he had the whole house to himself because his siblings were away at college, Damian tended to do his homework in his room.

"Are there any distractions in your room?" I asked Damian.

"Nope," he said earnestly.

I pressed him. "No television, no Xbox, no computer, no cell phone?"

"Well . . ." he began, and he didn't need to go any further. He didn't have to explain how difficult it was to avoid dashing off an instant message to a friend or how alluring it was to see his cell phone light up when he received a text message. Even though he didn't have a television in his room, he and I both knew that he could watch TV shows on his computer. He didn't need to explain all of this because I knew firsthand what he was going through.

"Actually," I confided to Damian, "I have to turn my cell phone off when I'm working or that little beep is all I hear."

He laughed knowingly, and we both knew the truth: his room, his sanctuary, was actually his enemy when it came to getting his homework done.

So for Damian, and most likely for your son, one of the most important first steps is finding a separate space in the house for him to do his homework, free of temptations. In Damian's case his family settled on the dining room, and each night he would go in and complete his homework block in the dining room, focused and free of distractions. When he was done with his work, he was able to relax in his room or do whatever else he pleased; because he now finished his homework much more quickly and effectively, he had more time to do things like work on model cars and ride his skateboard. His homework improved dramatically, as did his relationship with his parents!

Effective Study Spaces

One of the most important things parents can do to help their son is to create a consistent and calm study environment in the home. Remember, doing homework free of distractions doesn't necessarily mean doing homework alone in a cave. Different children have different needs. Some are independent and prefer complete and utter silence with not a single person within a hundred-foot radius, while others like to do homework with the comfort of knowing someone is sitting nearby or in the next room. You know your child best and can use these suggestions to adapt to the needs and structure of your home.

In the sections that follow, I offer some suggestions; I hope they will help you think about what would work in your home.

Dining Room

The dining room is my first choice for a consistent study space. If your house is like most, the dining room is one of the most underused spaces in the house—and it has a big empty table that makes the perfect workspace. There are typically few distractions there, and a dining room table provides ample workspace for a student to spread out his books and not feel cramped. In general, boys don't tend to associate their dining room with rest, relaxation, or anything else (this might not be the case if your dining room is used every night, but that isn't typical) and can usually complete their work there without distractions.

Of course, this assumes that you have a dining room and that it's free of the piles of stuff that sometimes accumulate in underused spaces. This may end up being an opportunity to organize your dining room as well, as long as that system doesn't interfere with what you set up for your son. The key, of course, is to keep distractions out of the dining room and create a quiet space—no music or cell phone during the homework block. I tell students to put their cell phone on silent in the other room

> I tell students to put their cell phone on silent in the other room so the dining room becomes a distraction-free zone.

so the dining room becomes a distraction-free zone. When students question me on this, I point out that they can check their messages and return calls when their homework is done.

Many parents ask me about computer use in the dining room, because most boys insist that they need their computer to complete their homework. I tell students to do whatever homework that does not involve a computer first, and then work on homework (an English essay, for example) that involves a computer. You can even go so far as disabling the Internet during the homework block (see Chapter 7) to help your son avoid the temptation of checking email, instant messaging, Facebook, YouTube, and whatever else distracts your son (sports, music, or college websites).

After a week of using the dining room, students often tell me how much more productive they were compared to when they were trying to study in their bedroom. Not only were they more productive but they were also more efficient, which gave them free time and enabled them to go to bed earlier.

Be aware, though, that like any other lifestyle change, there can be unintended consequences. A few years back, a parent called me and told me that her high school sophomore had fallen so in love with the system that he refused to do his homework in his room ever again, and his papers and books were now creating a mess in the dining room. This mom was happy that her son seemed to think he was more productive—but she was rightfully annoyed that her dining room had been infiltrated with papers, textbooks, and school supplies.

I asked if she had an empty shelf, or if she could create an empty space somewhere in or near the dining room where he could keep his supplies. A little grudgingly, she agreed, and set a rule that the dining room had to be cleaned up after his homework was done and everything put back into the dedicated shelf space. It was a fair and effective compromise; he was able to use his favorite study space, and his mom was able to have her dining room clean and empty at all other times.

Family Room/Kitchen

Maybe using the dining room is not an option in your home—perhaps you don't have a dining room, or the dining room table is a treasured family heirloom lacking protective covers. Maybe the layout of your home is such that people are constantly walking in and out of the dining room, which makes it less than ideal for a quiet, distraction-free sanctuary. In that case, perhaps the family room or kitchen table would be a better option.

A sixth grader I worked with who was the youngest in his family—he had an older sibling at college and another who was a junior in high school—really enjoyed doing his homework at the kitchen table while his mom was cooking dinner. That turned out to be a much more effective spot for him than his bedroom or the dining room, where he felt alone and anxious without someone nearby. Some children and teenagers like doing their homework when other people are around,

Some children and teenagers like doing their homework when other people are around, not necessarily as a distraction but as more of a comfort.

not necessarily as a distraction but of more of a comfort. His mom allowed him his space to do his work without making comments, and he completed his work without feeling alone.

The kitchen or family room are probably not good options if there is a lot of noise (such as a television on in the background) or if your child finds himself needing to get up every five minutes to get a snack or drink. For example, as a high school freshman Cole had three younger siblings and liked doing his homework in the kitchen because he liked to be in the middle of all the action. He loved being around his younger siblings—the youngest was a toddler—and his parents didn't immediately realize how distracting the kitchen was as the central family zone in their house.

When he switched to working in the dining room, he was able to close the door and find a quiet spot to focus and concentrate, and soon his eighth grade sister started successfully studying at the other end of the dining room table. I know it's not possible for all siblings to study effectively together, but for Cole and Amanda, it was actually easier to know that everyone was studying at the dining room table (on opposite sides) in a communal, quiet atmosphere.

Home Office

Some families have home offices that provide a separate space for their children to do homework. I am hesitant to give blanket approval of home offices, because as most of us know well, home offices can often have more than just a desk and a stapler. Most have computers with Internet access and a telephone, some have cast-off televisions that were once in the family room, and others are filled with financial information from the last five years that has yet to be properly filed. In other words, only you will know whether your home office is a good space to consider as the regular study space in the home. Home offices often have a door that can easily be shut to promote full concentration—which can be both a blessing and a curse. It's difficult for most teenagers to pry themselves from the temptations of instant messaging and Facebook; providing them with a space where they can shut the door and avoid accountability can be counterproductive.

Public Library

I was a high school junior when I discovered the amazing experience of getting heaps of work done at the public library. I started to go to my local branch to study for finals and found that after a few hours in the quiet section, I'd have completed what probably would have taken me the entire day to finish if I had stayed in my room. Indeed, using the public library in high school was also great training for college, where I quickly realized that freshman dorms have more distractions than any Internet or cell phone could ever provide. One of the advantages of using the library is that after students get their work done there, they can come home and completely relax.

> When I first suggest going to the library, students generally look a little skeptical.

When I first suggest going to the library, students generally look a little skeptical. A few ask me where the local library is. The library in our town happens to be right next to a few soccer fields where junior high and high school club teams practice in the evenings. More and more, some schools keep their libraries open for kids to use between school and afternoon sports practice, so using the school library during those times might also be a viable alternative.

Bill, a high school sophomore with whom I worked a few years back, had a terrible time prying himself away from computerized distractions. He had soccer practice on the fields next to the library two nights a week from 6:00 to 8:00, so those nights I suggested he get to the library right after school and work until around 5:30 to get most of his homework done before soccer practice. That way, he could come home after practice (when he was likely tired, sweaty, and cranky) and just take a shower and wind down. For the most part, the plan worked really well—there were a few nights when he wasn't quite able to get everything done at the library, but he was generally much more efficient and productive than if he had waited until later to start his homework.

Using the library on a daily basis may not be feasible for some students, who might live far away and not drive or who might have after-school activities that would make fitting in time for the library to be one thing too many in an already packed schedule. Remarkably, however, every student I have ever challenged to try to use the library three times a week (once on the weekend, and twice during the week) swears by the difference it made in getting work done and becoming more organized. The key is that they work in the quiet section and that they go by themselves or with one or two study buddies, but never more. Some students can efficiently study with a few friends around if they are each doing their own thing and collectively enjoy the company. Some friends, of course, are not the ones you want to take with you to the library because it would become a waste of time. The trick is to know which is which.

TIP: To encourage your child to get into the habit of going to the library, make it a weekend family tradition. I have seen this work well for both junior high and high school boys. Perhaps for a few hours on Saturday or Sunday afternoon, you both go to the library; he works on homework while you pay bills, answer emails, or simply read a book. The drive to and from the library can be a great time for simple conversations; library visits can turn into a nice natural bonding activity.

What If the Bedroom Is the Only Option?

In some homes, doing homework in the child's bedroom may be the only option. Perhaps there are lots of family members around and the dining room is constantly filled with people and activities. Or maybe there is no dining room and all other spaces in the home are filled. If the bedroom is truly the only option, here are a few things to think about to help your child create a homework space:

- *Help your child create a fresh start with a solid clean desk space.* Doing homework on the bed is a recipe for disaster, as noted earlier. The most important element of any desk is that it have a good amount of space where your student can effectively spread out his binder, books, and planner without feeling cramped. IKEA and Target are two places where you can find inexpensive, solid desk pieces, although assembly is often required.

- *Try to position the desk so it does not face the bed.* Can you imagine being tired and doing your homework while stealing furtive glances at your comfortable warm bed? Clearly a distraction for most tired preteens or teenagers. Some parents consult feng shui books such as Steven Post's *Modern Book of Feng Shui* to figure out the most effective layout for their child's bedroom and have found that helpful as well.

- *Avoid putting a desktop computer in the bedroom.* Many parents think they're doing their children a favor by putting a computer in their room, when in actuality, the computer quickly becomes part of the problem. First of all, a desktop computer on your son's desk takes up space and leaves him cramped when he needs to open his binder, read his textbook, and check his planner to get his science homework done. Having the computer in the bedroom also makes it difficult to escape distractions that computer-aided technology creates for many preteen and teenage boys. In the next chapter, I discuss tackling homework; students should do whatever homework requires the computer only *after* all other homework is done.

> Having the computer in the bedroom also makes it difficult to escape distractions that computer-aided technology creates for many preteen and teenage boys.

- *Have a designated place outside the bedroom where the student leaves his cell phone.* This tip is important no matter where your child does his homework, but it's even more important if he does his homework in his room. Have a box where phones are stored during homework time, similar to the place you put your keys each time you enter the house. Having a designated space is a great way to help children self-regulate. Have them put the phone on silent while they work in the other room. When they finish their work, they will have a complete update at their fingertips.

Creating That Home Space: Supplies and Other Necessities

Parents often ask me what materials children need for an effective home study space environment. There is no need to spend a lot of money, and you may already have most supplies around the house. The key is to put the supplies into one centralized location—perhaps create a bin or an organized box with all the school supplies—near the study area. If your child is doing homework in the dining room, perhaps there is a place to store these materials so they are within easy reach (and no longer require a fifteen-minute full-house search).

- Three-hole punch

- Binder paper: if possible, get binder paper with reinforced sides

- Reinforcements: for when the holes rip on the binder paper

- Index cards: buy these in bulk!

- Recipe boxes: to store the index cards

- An extra binder or two and extra dividers

- Miscellaneous: stapler, tape, scissors, glue stick, markers, construction paper, report covers

- Dictionary and thesaurus: I prefer to have actual tangible dictionaries rather than online computerized versions

Keep the supply box separate from your own supplies, and have your son check it on the first Sunday evening of the month to see if any supplies need to be replenished.

Final Thoughts

As a parent, you can take ownership of one of the critical elements in helping your son find his own success: helping him to create a consistent, calm study environment. Many preteen and teenage boys cannot verbalize the importance of a separate study space until they have one that feels comfortable. *Another note:* Sometimes students will find they need a change of scenery. While I generally write at my desk in my home, sometimes I write at my office or in the big armchair in my living room; there is

> Many preteen and teenage boys cannot verbalize the importance of a separate study space until they have one that feels comfortable.

nothing wrong with having a few regular spots as long as an overall pattern of good study skills is established. So perhaps your son likes the public library some days and the dining room table on others. Each child is different; finding the right balance takes time.

Summary

While I have preferences for certain rooms over others, the bottom line for an effective study space is one that provides the most peace of mind (and necessary supplies) with the fewest distractions. For some kids, this will mean a common space, such as a dining room, that has been modified in some way that's acceptable to all. For others it may mean the public library. I generally don't recommend bedrooms for studying because of the many inherent distractions, but if that is the only option, do your best to balance those temptations with a defined and properly supplied space within which your child can concentrate.

7

Scheduling Homework to Manage Time Effectively

When students come to my office, I ask them to hand over their cell phone at the beginning of each visit. I put the phone aside, on silent, where it patiently waits until the end of our session. Inevitably, when I give the phone back, there are an assortment of new text messages and phone calls waiting to be digested. It's no secret that today's kids are technologically tuned in like no generation before; the combination of cell phones, Internet access, instant messaging, and social networking sites creates an environment full of distractions and free of limitations. Indeed, many students who come into my office convinced that they're overwhelmed by the number of hours spent studying are unable to recognize how those one-minute breaks here or five-minute chats derail them from getting work done efficiently.

Any parent who has worked in an office knows how easy it is to create distractions sitting at a desk. Shopping online? Catching up with an old friend on the phone? Instant messaging your spouse to find out what to do about dinner? Before I worked with high school students, I was an investment-banking analyst at a large firm. At our office, we were usually in the office around 8:30 a.m., even though our superiors generally didn't give our work assignments for the day until around 3:00 or 4:00 p.m., and we would spend all night creating Excel spreadsheets and PowerPoint presentations, and printing way too many financial documents. How did we spend our morning hours? I shopped and paid bills online, a few of my colleagues were active members of a fantasy baseball league, and we all spent more than a few minutes talking long-distance to our friends working similar jobs in other offices. An outside observer might think we were hard at work, but the reality was something quite different.

I have seen students increase their efficiency and effectiveness by scheduling their homework and creating a routine. As a result, their work is of higher quality *and* they have more time to spend doing whatever else they please. As parents, you can play a major role in helping them create and maintain that routine. Think about the message you are sending in your home. Is the television always on in the evenings? Might you consistently designate a few hours every evening as quiet time, during which everyone in the house could work on something that's valued?

> Think about the message you are sending in your home. Is the television always on in the evenings?

When Mark first walked into my office, he looked exhausted. Tall and athletic, he was a motivated student who wanted to do well but appeared stressed. Even though his grades were strong, he seemed anxious and overwhelmed. "I'm doing homework six to seven hours a night," he complained. "I don't get to bed before one or two in the morning."

I casually asked him where he did his homework, and he replied that he did it at the desk in his room.

"Is your computer on when you are doing your homework?" I asked.

"Sure—I need my computer to do my homework."

"What about AIM? Is that on?"

"Yeah, but no one is really on. Just once in a while."

"Where is your cell phone?"

"In my pocket."

"What about your music?"

"You can't do homework without music. It's, like, illegal."

Mark and I made a deal: For one week, he would do his homework, uninterrupted, at the dining room table. He would put his cell phone on silent in the other room, forget music, and do homework or assignments requiring his computer last. He would also disable his computer's instant messaging program during homework time.

A week later, he came into my office, sheepishly converted. "You were right, I got so much more done. The first two days were tough. I wanted to turn on my music, and I even did on the second day. But I noticed how much more I got done, and went to bed before 10:30 every night, even with soccer practice."

Study Habits That Work *and* Free Up Time

In Chapter 6, I talked about creating a consistent space to study, which ideally is away from the bedroom. In addition to physical space, it's also important to create a set block of time to complete homework and other school-related tasks. When setting up homework blocks, keep in mind the following parameters.

Schedule Homework Time

On Sunday afternoons, students should look at their week and schedule their homework time on their planner. After looking at his schedule and figuring in soccer practice, guitar lessons, or a math

As parents, you can encourage a set homework schedule by creating time (either before or after dinner) when everyone works on tasks free of technological distractions.

tutor, boys should schedule their homework time blocks. This helps them become more proactive and reduces anxiety and procrastination. As parents, you can encourage a set homework schedule by creating time (either before or after dinner) when everyone works on tasks free of technological distractions. You could do some bill paying or read a book or newspaper, and your children could work on homework and related assignments.

Set a Break Time Before Starting Homework

Many boys already spend eight hours a day chained to their desk at school, where they are admonished for getting up, fidgeting, and otherwise creating distractions. In fact, far too many schools limit any kind of movement (including stretching!) to recess and are even cutting way back on that essential activity. By the time these boys get home, the last thing they want to do is sit still and stare at homework. I encourage boys who come home right after school to take a short break, get a snack, sit down and read a magazine, or do something active such as shooting a few baskets, playing with the dog in the backyard, or even juggling with a Hacky Sack (a surprising stress reliever!) before starting their homework, for both their mental and physical well-being. The caveat is that for some boys, going online or watching

I encourage boys who come home right after school to take a short break, get a snack, sit down and read a magazine, or do something active such as shooting a few baskets, playing with the dog in the backyard, or even juggling with a Hacky Sack . . . before starting their homework.

TV is a black hole, so leaving that for *after* the homework block is key.

TIP: Some boys have tremendous difficulty refocusing on schoolwork once they take a break. This is especially true for students who are easily distracted or who struggle with transitions. If that sounds like your son, keep the after-school break to a bare minimum, with time to eat a snack and take a few minutes to get organized before starting his work.

When Paul, our Seriously Struggling Student, first came into my office, he seemed discouraged and overwhelmed. He really wanted to do well and spent the greater part of every afternoon doing schoolwork. As soon as he got home, he sat down and opened his backpack and began his work. He didn't even take a break for a snack or to rest—he just ate while working. Because his processing speed was in the 13th percentile, assignments generally took him longer; he accepted that and allotted extra time for himself. But the problem was, he wasn't taking a mental break from sitting down and doing work, and so he became drained and felt completely unengaged in the learning process. To Paul, each day after school signaled another cycle of unending work.

One of the first things I asked Paul was what he enjoyed doing in his spare time; he looked at me incredulously and replied, "What spare time?" After much prodding, he described a budding interest in photography. He wasn't actively involved in anything at school, in part because he was always worried about completing his work and receiving good grades. So

> He wasn't actively involved in anything at school, in part because he was always worried about completing his work and receiving good grades.

I suggested that he take a solid hour off after coming home from school and use that time to do something relaxing. If he built in even a half hour to spend on something active three times a week—going for a run, riding his bike, or spending time outside taking photographs—before sitting down to do his homework, he could clear his mind after sitting at a desk all day and reenergize himself before starting his homework.

Within six weeks, there was a noticeable difference in Paul's approach to his schoolwork. Even though it still took him longer than most of his peers to complete his homework (because he listened to most of his textbooks on tape), he scheduled blocks of homework with a complete break. Slowly, he began to feel more in control of his schoolwork, and he began to really enjoy his outside interests, instead of being focused solely on school. When he did focus on his work, he felt better able to concentrate and more positive about the amount of time he was spending because he could take a break and recharge before delving in.

Schedule Two-Hour Homework Blocks

For most kids, the idea of a two-hour homework block seems manageable, because, I point out to them, if they start at 4:30, they can be done by 7:00 even if they take a solid ten-minute break after every half hour of work. By 7:00, they are done with all their schoolwork and have the rest of the evening to themselves to do whatever they please. Most students who walk into my office complain that they are never done before midnight, so the idea of getting done so early is highly motivating. Being done by 7:00 and having the rest of the evening free is the reward that motivates them.

> Most students who walk into my office complain that they are never done before midnight, so the idea of getting done so early is highly motivating.

118 ■

I encourage high school students to do a two-hour block of homework Monday through Thursday, and then schedule two two-hour blocks sometime between Friday, Saturday, and Sunday. The caveat is that both weekend two-hour blocks cannot be done on Sunday, because the whole idea of having set homework times is to be proactive rather than reactive, and sitting down on Sunday evening at 8:00 to start four hours of homework seems like the worst way to get ready for a new school week. Instead, students can do two hours on Saturday from 11:00 a.m. to 1:00 p.m. and another two-hour block on Sunday from 3:00 to 5:00 p.m. They have the rest of the time to spend time with friends, go to the movies, play video games, or whatever else they may want to do.

Some students who have a rigorous course load or who generally take longer to complete assignments might have more than two hours of homework. If that is the case, encourage a complete thirty- to sixty-minute break between homework blocks. In an ideal world, your son would be able to do something physically active or relaxing during that break; even just getting up and moving around will make him better able to focus when he sits down and gets back to work.

FAQ: HOMEWORK TIME

1. My son is in junior high. Is two hours appropriate?

It depends on your son's classes, the expectations of the school, and how long it takes him to get work done. Schools, in general, assign ten minutes of homework per grade level, so a seventh grader has about an hour and ten minutes worth of homework per night. But that varies—a student taking advanced math and a foreign language might easily have close to two hours. Two hours is a good bet for most junior high and younger high school students.

2. What if my son does not have two hours of homework every night?

The two-hour block is not just for homework—it is also a time when students can make flash cards, complete review sheets, read upcoming chapters in their biology book—anything that helps them become more proactive in their schoolwork. In Chapter 8, I discuss long-term strategies for studying; your son can work on some of those strategies to fill his two-hour block of time. By doing two hours of homework on a consistent basis, even on the nights students think they have only ten minutes of written homework, will eliminate or greatly reduce the chances of having a night with seven hours of homework, when they are staring bleary-eyed and frustrated at the computer at two in the morning.

Do Homework Before Technological Distractions

Recently, I started working with a high school freshman named Adam, who is sweet and affable and looks far younger than his fifteen years. When we first met, he was really excited because he had a friend who had worked with me who said that I had "completely changed her life." So, needless to say, he was incredibly enthusiastic and very honest about his challenges getting homework done. He told me that because he did not have an after-school activity, he came home every day around 3:30 and sat down at his desk but didn't actually start his homework until 8:00 or 9:00. Despite giving the appearance of diligently working on his homework at his computer desk, he was clearly up to something else, and it didn't take long for him to reveal the truth.

Despite giving the appearance of diligently working on his homework at his computer desk, he was clearly up to something else, and it didn't take long for him to reveal the truth.

"When I come home," he told me, "I get a snack and go up to my room and get on the Internet on Facebook and AIM until about 8:00. Then I have dinner and try to start my homework, but by then I am exhausted."

"Of course you are," I told him. "Staring at the computer screen for that long will do that to you. But, seriously, four hours of Facebook?"

"I know," he said sheepishly. "But once I start, I'm just sucked in. There is always someone new, and now that a lot of the kids that I went to junior high with go to different high schools, it's our way of keeping in touch."

I explained to Adam how draining staring at a computer screen can be, and we agreed that if he was coming home right after school, he should do his homework from 4:00 to 6:00 downstairs, and then by 6:30, the night would be his to do whatever he pleased. To Adam, the important thing was that I wasn't taking away his ability to spend time on the computer. I was simply changing the sequence.

Over the next few weeks, Adam made the transition to doing his homework first and then going upstairs to spend his typical hours on the Internet. He did feel much more relaxed now that he could get his homework done and didn't have to stay up late worrying about whether he was going to finish in time. But we didn't stop there. Once Adam felt like he had made the successful transition to doing his homework before jumping on the computer, I convinced him to start using a kitchen timer to track his time on Facebook.

"At first, give yourself a whole hour," I said. "Go to all the sites you want, leave messages on people's walls, send emails, whatever. Concentrate your time on the computer so that what you once spent four hours doing you can now get done in an hour." Over time, he weaned himself and now spends only about thirty minutes a day getting everything he wants out of Facebook, AIM, and other social networking sites.

After the Homework Block, Give Free Reign (Within Reason)

Often, when I first meet a student, I emphasize that once he is done with his two-hour block of homework, the night is young and the night is *his*; instead of feeling chained to his desk, he can relax, unwind, and focus on whatever he enjoys. He'll have time to spend on the phone, instant messaging, playing the guitar, or whatever else he finds relaxing and fun. It's important for parents to remember that many boys feel a need to stay included in the social networking scene (from email to Facebook), which they feel they're missing out on during homework time.

In essence, the freedom to do what they want is the crucial reward and motivation that keeps students wanting to be efficient and organized. My main message is not that students should study all the time and not do anything fun, it's that they should maximize and focus their efforts so they have more time for fun and outside activities. Even if their grades don't magically improve overnight, they should still get to do what they want after they've finished their agreed-on homework blocks. Again, focusing on the study habits rather than the grades will promote greater long-term success.

> In essence, the freedom to do what they want is the crucial reward and motivation that keeps students wanting to be efficient and organized.

Reduce or Eliminate Multi-Tasking

When I made the deal with Mark that led to his turnaround in productivity, I explained that for every instant message or phone call that comes in while he is trying to do his homework or studying, he can easily get off track for five to fifteen minutes, stretching about an hour and a half of solid work into an exhausting six hours at his desk. If he had two hours of uninterrupted time, he would likely get more done, and hence be available much earlier to go back online, if that was how he chose to spend his spare time.

Even though the idea is ultimately to eliminate multi-tasking and distractions, I say *reduce* multi-tasking because I recognize that it is a process, and the typical boy cannot go from multiple distractions to none in a single day. Distractions from cell phones and computers can be reduced right away by making them less available. So recognize that it is a process over time and that slip-ups might occur, but encourage your son to be as distraction free as possible. Once he sees the benefits of how much he can get done in less time, he will be more willing to make the long-term changes, but he may need reminders now and again, and consistency is key.

FAQ: MULTI-TASKING

1. What if my son needs to use the computer for school?

Many students insist that they need to use a computer for school, and indeed, in many schools computer use is a mandatory part of the curriculum. In general, I recommend that students do all their homework that does *not* require the use of the computer first, and then tackle whatever needs the computer. And, of course, the goal is for them not to have instant messaging programs or web browsers open when they are typing up their essay for history class.

2. My son insists he needs music to study. Is that okay?

Many of us enjoy listening to music as we go about our day, whether it's while we drive, jog, clean the house, or sit in a doctor's waiting room. It is interesting that researchers who have found that distractions in general are bad for concentration and learning are loathe to include music in that category as long as it makes schoolwork more enjoyable. If your son insists that music puts him in a relaxed and open frame of mind while studying, insist that it be instrumental music only—classical or instrumental jazz, for instance, which are less likely than rock or other kinds of lyrical music to cause a significant distraction. After successfully switching from lyrical to instrumental music, the next step would be to eliminate music altogether.

TIP: Some students who find themselves uncomfortable in total silence have found that white noise machines can be helpful in creating a relaxing atmosphere without the distraction that comes from listening to their favorite bands while trying to figure out math problems.

Encourage Structured Breaks

I have worked with many boys who, for a variety of reasons, think that two hours is a ridiculous amount of time to have to sit still *to do homework*. (Some of these same children spend five hours straight playing video games.) Here is a strategy that works well: Instead of doing two hours straight, break it into four chunks of thirty minutes each or three chunks of forty-five minutes apiece. Use a kitchen timer, and have them focus for thirty or forty-five minutes, and then give them ten minutes to get up, walk around, go to the bathroom, get a snack, fidget—whatever they would be doing that would help them procrastinate. *Note:* When they take a ten-minute break, allow them to do anything as long as it doesn't involve technology. The moment they flip on their cell phone, check instant messaging, or open their web browser, ten minutes will turn into three hours before they know it.

> The moment they flip on their cell phone, check instant messaging, or open their web browser, ten minutes will turn into three hours before they know it.

Once your son feels comfortable doing concentrated work for thirty minutes at a time, see if he can extend it to forty or forty-five, and go from there. I have worked with many students who are diagnosed with ADD/ADHD, and this strategy has worked well for them. Most of the boys like the use of the kitchen timer (and it helps them keep their breaks to only ten minutes long).

Create a Technology Box

According to the Nielsen company, in the fall of 2008, U.S. teenagers averaged 1,742 text messages sent or received *per month*, a statistic that doesn't surprise me at all. One of the boys with whom I worked told me he sent and received 20,000 text messages during October of his freshman year. I tried to figure out how that was mathematically feasible, and it was difficult—he must have been texting while eating and sleeping, even if some of the text message conversations probably went something like this:

QT1: Hey
URSon2: Hey
QT1: whz up?
URSon2: Doin HW—u?
QT1: Cool me 2—sucks

Regardless, this family knew that text messaging had overtaken the kids' lives, so they created a technology box in the front of the house. Each boy places his phone and music device in a simple, nicely adorned large box with a cover, during homework time, and gets it back when he is done. They lock their phones and put them on silent before they put them in the technology box, so their messages are waiting for them when they retrieve it after finishing their homework.

Encourage Your Son to Filter His Outside Activities

Recently, a family came in to talk with me about their son's college application process. We started talking about all the activities their son was involved in; it turned out he was the epitome of an Over-Scheduled Procrastinator, with soccer, student government, a rock band, a girlfriend, and various clubs eating up all his time and making him feel overwhelmed and slightly anxious. In talking to me, the parents admitted that they were also very involved in everything when they were in high school, so they could understand his dilemma.

"When you were both in high school I bet the time commitment for each of these activities was less than it is now," I surmised. Both parents nodded in agreement and started to recognize the difference. The truth is, being on the soccer team in the twenty-first century rarely just involves showing up for two practices and a game every week—there is conditioning, weight training, multiple-hour practices, and far-away weekend tournaments. Similarly, serving on student government, depending on your son's school, might require two meetings a week and multiple evening events every month. And a rock band? Well, there are practices, jam sessions, and playing at talent shows and local gigs. The opportunities for scheduling challenges are endless.

> Encourage your son to become engaged in activities that are meaningful to him, and concentrate on those interests while being open to new opportunities and adventures.

Encourage your son to become engaged in activities that are meaningful to him, and concentrate on those interests while being open to new opportunities and adventures. At the same time, help him be mindful of not overcommitting himself (see Chapter 9), which means he will be unable to do anything to the degree he would like. Getting home at 9:00 or 10:00 every night is a recipe for an exhausted, low-functioning young person—one who sadly loses out on the fun and rewarding aspects of all the activities he's putting time into.

Summary

So much of what makes a homework routine efficient revolves around scheduling. Not only should homework time be consistently scheduled (same starting and ending time every night), but the breaks and endpoints need to be consistent as well. Timers work well in this regard; don't forget to use devices such as technology boxes for storing distracting cell phones and computer-free periods that remove the temptation to check social media sites.

Also remember that while you may need to segregate study time from play time, it's important to give your child free reign to indulge himself in personal activities (appropriately, of course) once that scheduled study time is complete. To make the goal of being better organized and managing time more effectively a win–win situation, boys need to feel that they will get time to relax and enjoy themselves once the workday is over.

8

Strategies for Quizzes, Tests, Projects, and Finals

The scene is familiar to many parents: it's 11:00, the night before some big project is due. The project was, of course, assigned a week or month ago, and the teacher gave explicit instructions to work on it ahead of time, but in the rush of life, activities, video games, and friends, it never seemed to be a huge issue. Really, it seemed to be more of a secondary thought, until the night before it is due. Depending on your son's style, the night before can be a time of intense procrastination, severe panic, or happy-go-lucky "Hmmm ... that project worth 10 percent of our grade is due tomorrow. Where is that assignment sheet again?"

Some parents become frustrated and angry at the whole process, while others are more detached, as in, "Well, he will need to face the consequences." Many of the parents I talk with secretly become involved in helping with the project or essay or studying for the test, often because they just want their son to be done with the assignment so he can go to bed, and they can all finally get some rest.

Perhaps you are a bit skeptical about how you could get your son to start working ahead on his long-term assignments, quizzes, tests, projects, and essays. And why not? Many adults are resigned to doing things at the last minute, and in so doing, end up just wanting to get it done (as opposed to wanting to do it well). Many people function this way, whether they like it or not, relying on the adrenaline rush that comes with cutting things down to the wire. What they often don't recognize is that this constant rush wears us down.

Instead, consider the comfort and confidence that comes from feeling in control, on top of things, and successful. Perhaps your son has not felt that sense of confidence yet in his life, or it has been a long time since he has felt that he was performing at his personal best. When boys feel that sense of confidence and self-assuredness a few times, it becomes addictive, just like getting to the next level of a video game or striving to become a starter on the sports team. It's that same competition high—except they are competing against themselves and enjoying the feeling of mastery when they do it well.

> When boys feel that sense of confidence and self-assuredness a few times, it becomes addictive, just like getting to the next level of a video game or striving to become a starter on the sports team.

In this chapter, I outline strategies for helping your son learn to prepare for quizzes, tests, and finals as well as how to successfully complete long-term assignments such as projects and essays. Each school and teacher is different, with different requirements and ways of presenting material, so although some of the strategies I outline here will be useful just as they are for your son, others may need to be tweaked a bit to work for his needs. The strategies I present have been helpful for students from a wide variety of academic abilities and backgrounds and are ways to learn how to study and master material.

There are different strategies for helping boys study for different types of quizzes (math, history, science) and this chapter has tips on how to help them learn the material as well as strategies to schedule and prepare themselves for final exams. A formatted scheduling tool for final exams is provided on page 159.

Depending on your son's age (junior high or high school) and your relationship and communication styles, you may or may not be able to help him implement all of these strategies. However, there are many ways to help your son understand and appreciate how to use his time more effectively to get better grades. Even if he adopts just the two-hour block of time to get ahead on longer-term assignments and study for tests and quizzes (rather than cramming at the last minute), he will have a significant incremental change that over time will show real results.

TIP: Right now you might be wondering how to present all the information in this chapter to your son. Well, not all at once, I hope! When students come into my office, I give them tips and suggestions for how to study for assignments, quizzes, or tests that are coming up. When they have a long-term project, we sit down and map out strategies, and I help them create their own detailed game plan (this is also true for writing essays or studying for final exams). If I tried to give this information to students all at once, they would turn around and walk out the door, overwhelmed and unmotivated. Use this chapter as a resource and a guide to help your son devise and implement strategies over time, as the school year unfolds.

Proactive vs. Reactive

One of the key advantages for the preteen and adolescent boys with whom I work is that they quickly see how much less stressful their lives are when they become proactive rather than reactive. The set block of time that I discuss in Chapter 7 (scheduled consistently every night, Monday through Thursday, with two blocks scheduled somewhere between Friday and Sunday) is important not only because it ensures that they finish their nightly homework but also because it gives boys the set time and space to work ahead on their assignments. As I mentioned in Chapter 7, with my students, the scheduled block of time actually *decreases* stress and anxiety. Because the boys know when they are going to work on homework, they are not worried about when and how they are going to get around to studying for that exam or finishing that paper that is due on Monday.

Let me explain it this way: Say there is a long-term project assigned that will, in all likelihood, take six hours to complete successfully (this also can apply to studying for big exams). If the work is spread out over four ninety-minute chunks, it will be less stressful and more efficient for several reasons. First, it's a fact that after about two hours of working on something without a break, most people become restless and need to step away. By starting something the night before it's due, your son won't have time for the natural breaks he's going to need, and that produces more stress and lowers the quality of his work.

Also, very few students can shut out the world for an entire evening; after all, we're talking about the same boy whose phone fills up with text messages and whose Facebook page has a place in the center of his world. With all of his breaks scheduled in advance, he's happy to know there will be a chance to reply to a few texts and Facebook posts, particularly if there's something social going on that might be a distraction at the back of his mind.

Last, every project has its unexpected problems and roadblocks. By spacing out the work, your son will build in the time to handle any setbacks that often add to stress and deadline worries.

> By starting something the night before it's due, your son won't have time for the natural breaks he's going to need, and that produces more stress and lowers the quality of his work.

You might think that this argument will fall on deaf ears, but remember what I mentioned before about presenting these concepts to your son as *win–win propositions*. By spreading the work out, he can spend *less* overall time on the project and do much better on it, while keeping his stress levels to a minimum.

Designate Break Times

One of the reasons that kids avoid starting to study for big tests or complete long-term projects is that they see it as a long, black tunnel of work with no end in sight. At the office, most adults take breaks throughout the day—a coworker stopping at their desk, a meeting or lunch appointment. Sitting at the dining room table in front of his school materials with no end in sight is torturous for any middle school or adolescent boy—and something he would likely avoid at all costs.

Not only is it important to break up the projects and preparation into smaller manageable tasks, it is also crucial to create breaks when kids can do something fun and stress relieving. Time the breaks so that for every few hours spent studying (with little five-minute breaks here and there to get up and move around) they have twenty to thirty minutes to completely free their minds and do something entirely unrelated to school. Anything outdoors is preferable when that is an option, including playing fetch with the dog or tossing the baseball around with a neighbor.

Active vs. Passive Learning

Many of the strategies I highlight in this chapter rely on the idea that active learning is more effective—and more likely to engage your son—than passive learning. During active learning, your son is busy under-

> During active learning your son is busy underlining, highlighting, making notes in the margins, creating his own flash cards and review sheets, and generally developing systems by which he can *help himself* learn the material without relying solely on rote memory.

lining, highlighting, making notes in the margins, creating his own flash cards and review sheets, and generally developing systems by which he can *help himself* learn the material without relying solely on rote memory. *Note:* Whereas girls will often have five different colors to outline, circle, box, underline, and highlight, boys generally just want a pencil or pen to underline.

Active learning keeps your son engaged longer, because he'll be actively working to create his study aids rather than merely looking at a sheet of paper and hoping he can remember the information when the test comes around.

How to Handle Quizzes

Depending on your child's teacher or class, he may have only a few quizzes here and there or have quite a few on a regular basis. Learning the material to do well on quizzes is a great foundational tool to help students learn incrementally, so they do not feel overwhelmed when big tests or final exams come around.

Reading Quizzes

Many students mistakenly think that if they are given a reading quiz on Wednesday, they should do all the reading on Tuesday night so that it is fresh in their minds. For a rare few students (my college classmate with the photographic memory, for instance) that system will work well. The rest—the vast majority of students—should spend the night before going over what they have already read and reviewing it, rather than reading it for the first time. As a general guideline, if students are given several nights to read the material, they should spend the first few nights reading and use the night before to review, rather than reading the material for the first time.

FAQ: AUDIOBOOKS

1. Is using audiobooks appropriate?

Sometimes parents (and kids) think that audiobooks are cheating; I don't share that view. As far as I'm concerned, how the material gets into your son's brain—whether through the eyes by reading or through the ears by listening—isn't important; *comprehension* is the key. Just because we've used printed materials for thousands of years doesn't make that the only worthwhile medium for learning. (Indeed, before the printed word, there was the oral tradition, which is how information and stories were passed down through the generations for many centuries.) If your son prefers to listen to a novel rather than read it, by all means let him absorb the material that way. Generally, I find it best when students who use audiobooks are also following along by looking at the book—it allows them to underline information they think is important and take notes as appropriate.

Some Tips to Help with Reading Quizzes

- Encourage your son to treat reading assignments like every other type of homework and complete them during the home-work block.

- He should complete his reading at a table or sitting on a comfy chair, but not sprawled half asleep on the coach or bed.

- Encourage him to read *actively*; underlining and taking notes in the margin if he is allowed to write in the book. If not, you can either photocopy chapters or have your son mark important information on sticky notes attached to the page.

- Let him use reading guides or summaries as a tool to aid comprehension, when necessary. I am not opposed to using SparkNotes or CliffsNotes or some other resource as a supplement so a student can get the basic plot of tougher, more dense literature, especially when a student struggles with English. I have found that knowing the basic plot can help students become more engaged, which helps them get more out of the reading. The key is, your son must read the actual book plus underline and take notes on whatever he thinks is important.

> After finishing reading, the student should take five minutes to jot down some plot-based points on the reading: what happened, to whom, where, when, and why.

- After finishing reading, the student should take five minutes to jot down some plot-based points on the reading: what happened, to whom, where, when, and why. By spending five to ten minutes right after he is done reading, he will save himself time later on and be better able to retain the information.

Vocabulary Quizzes

The key to vocabulary quizzes is very simple—creating flash cards. This works with vocabulary words for foreign language classes as well. I know there are teachers who really think that folding one side of a word list (where one side of the page has the word, and the other side has the definition) works just as well, but I tend to disagree. In my experience, students are more likely to be engaged if they are actively learning, and flipping flash cards is more active than staring at a word list. For best results, have your son place the word on one side and the definition on the other side. On the side with the definition, also have him write his own sentence that uses the word in context.

TIP: The famous book *Word Power Made Easy* by Norman Lewis is well used and well loved by grammar and English aficionados, and it is a great resource for learning the roots of vocabulary.

Math Quizzes

There are two important things for your son to do when reviewing for a math quiz or test—and they are actually quite simple:

1. He should start by creating his own review sheet of all the formulas, terms, and other necessary information. Again, this is *active* learning. Going through the book and/or class notes to pull out all the important formulas and create a review sheet is the best way to start thinking about the formulas and to begin understanding why and how they work.

2. Then he should create a pretest and do practice problems, making sure to understand and correct any mistakes. Many students think that just looking at their notes and going over their homework will be sufficient to be ready for a quiz. Wrong. Actually redoing problems takes less time and is more effective and gives your son the confidence that he knows how to solve the problems before he takes the quiz.

Map Quizzes

There is a simple way to improve performance on map quizzes, those that focus on geography and memorizing states, countries, capitals, and bodies of water. The student should print out ten blank copies of the map and the list of all the geographical terms he is responsible for learning for the quiz. Then, he should fill in the first copy from memory. Once he has that as a baseline, he should use each of the other nine copies as practice tests, filling in each one and then going back to the original to fill in what he missed.

There are also a lot of free online resources for teaching kids maps. If the map quiz is going to be a written quiz, I still suggest using the blank map technique, but this can be supplemented by using the online map games, which many students find engaging.

Foreign Language Quizzes

Many parents make the mistake of thinking that because they do not speak the language their child is studying in school, there is no way they can help their child study that language. In actuality, just flipping flash cards (see the next section) and helping him learn his vocabulary can make a big difference, and having him correct your incorrect pronunciation can be both helpful and engaging. After all, why not have a few laughs at your expense?

The Indispensable Flash Card

Flash cards are one of the best ways to help students learn material. My students inevitably balk at the idea of having to make flash cards ("Writing them all down will take *so* long!" is a common refrain), but once they ace a tough quiz or test in a class in which they were struggling, they find themselves grudgingly agreeing with me. Flash cards are compact, easy to carry around, and allow students to focus on what they actually *do* and *do not* know—something simply looking at notes and rereading the material does not allow for. This is especially true for those who struggle with memorization. I am not suggesting that students substitute rote memory for actual learning, but I am saying that flash cards are one of the many tricks to help improve material mastery.

In my office, I often show students my simple trick for learning a stack of flash cards quickly, accurately, and relatively painlessly:

1. Learn five flash cards. Take a few minutes to *really* learn them.

2. Then add five more, and review all ten.

3. After all ten are reviewed, add five more, and review all fifteen.

Ideally, someone (a sibling, friend, parent) can quiz the student after he learns five, ten, or fifteen flash cards. Students are often amazed at how fast they can almost effortlessly learn an entire stack of cards and really become confident with the information. This works for vocabulary quizzes, history tests, biology terms, and many other subject areas.

> Students are often amazed at how fast they can almost effortlessly learn an entire stack of cards and really become confident with the information.

TIP: After your child makes flash cards for an upcoming quiz or test, store them away in a recipe box or shoe box. Get a box for each subject, and keep all old flash cards in them. That way, when finals or a big test come up, he can just go through and pull out the ones he has already made rather than having to make new ones.

Big Tests

Ah, the big test; the one that covers three chapters, or two months' worth of information, or somewhere in between. Points earned on big tests can have nearly as much impact on your son's grade as the final exam. The following sections outline some key points.

Is There a Review Sheet?

In addition to telling students what chapter or section the test will cover, many teachers give some form of review sheet in advance of upcoming tests. It surprises many parents to find out that their son does not realize how to take advantage of the review sheet. I cannot tell you how many times I encounter freshman or sophomore boys who think it sufficient to just peruse a review sheet that has fifty or more terms on it. For those rare students who have a brilliant working memory, that strategy might be enough. For the rest of us, actually answering all the questions on the review sheet and learning all the pertinent information is one of the best ways to start the studying process.

If the teacher does not hand out a review sheet, your son can create and compile his own review sheet using notes, the book, information from quizzes, and other sources. In doing so, he is actively identifying the material he needs to master.

The Review Sheet Is Only Half the Battle

Tony was a diligent, hardworking student who always completed the history review sheets, though he would typically start doing them at 9:00 the night before the exam. He figured that simply writing down all the answers was sufficient to do well on the exams. But by the time he accomplished this, it would be around midnight, and Tony was exhausted and ready to go to bed—*not* ready to begin learning all the information he just spent three hours collecting. In the end, he became frustrated and was ready to give up, convinced that even after he'd studied to the point of exhaustion, he was still doing poorly.

What Tony did not realize was that he needed to complete the review sheet (either the one given out by the teacher or one of his own making) *at least two nights before the test*. Once he started to finish everything at least two nights before, he spent the night before the tests relaxed and prepared to flip flash cards, go over anything that was really confusing him, and generally develop the feeling of being prepared and confident. This preparation translated into a dramatic increase in his performance on tests, which further increased his confidence in his own abilities.

Flip Flash Cards the Night Before the Test

After your son puts the important information on flash cards a few nights ahead of time, help him spend the night before the test reviewing the cards. The great thing about putting the information on flash cards is that your son can then go through and identify what he really knows and what he still needs to learn. That way, he filters and focuses on the material he still needs to learn, instead of just staring at notes on a page or paragraphs in a book.

Create a Practice Test

Plays have dress rehearsals, soccer teams have scrimmages, and students should give themselves practice tests to prepare for the real thing. Encourage your son to devise a practice test using questions from the review sheet or math problems from the book (a foolproof method is to choose problems from the book for which there are answers in the back). He can also do this on his own or with a classmate: They each create a practice test for the other, and by doing so will get double the amount of practice, because they'll be creating *and* answering questions.

A Word About Test Anxiety

Many students perform below their true academic potential on exams because of high levels of test anxiety. Many of the strategies in this chapter will help your son feel more confident and less panicked in testing situations, because he will finally feel prepared and in control.

This common, and sometimes overwhelming, anxiety is one of the reasons that parental attitude, as discussed in Chapter 2, is such a crucial factor for your son to make progress on being organized, managing his time, and feeling successful both inside and outside the classroom. In fact, studies directly link parental pressure to test anxiety. If your son is met with comments like, "Why can't you learn?" or "Well, you must not have been paying attention!" he is likely to retreat even further.

Testing anxiety is real. If your child is struggling on tests even when he has mastered the material beforehand, talk with him about how he feels when he takes a big test. Also, encourage him to be proactive and speak with his teacher about his testing anxiety; many teachers will help students come up with classroom solutions that may help alleviate some of their concerns. Some common symptoms of testing anxiety include the following:

- Having headaches, stomachaches

- Sweating, feeling short of breath

- Feeling helpless, dreading school

- Avoiding school, regularly becoming sick on test days

- Having difficulty concentrating, feeling as though his mind went blank

- Fidgeting, pacing back and forth

> Encourage him to be proactive and speak with his teacher about his testing anxiety; many teachers will help students come up with classroom solutions that may help alleviate some of their concerns.

- Unable to sleep the night before tests

- Loss of appetite

When I was interning at a junior high school, I co-led a testing anxiety group run by the school psychologist. The small group had a good number of boys, many of whom were initially reluctant to share their stories about being nervous (that whole tough-guy scenario), but when they started sharing their feelings of being overwhelmed, it became clear to me that many boys are quick to give up and would prefer to appear ambivalent rather than confront their fears of failure.

The goal of our testing anxiety group was that each student come away with one or two strategies that he could employ to help him on a regular basis. Six sessions later, the students felt more relaxed and confident when they sat down to take their tests, thanks to the basic techniques outlined next.

Most boys are not likely to volunteer the fact that they get nervous or scared in testing situations. But with a bit of gentle questioning, you can determine if that is the case for your child, and if so, you can incorporate the following strategies into his test-prep routine.

Visualize

A few nights before every test, and particularly the night before, have him visualize what he is going to do when the test is placed in front of him. He should visualize the test going really well, with him feeling relaxed, confident, and in control.

Thirty Seconds, Five Deep Breaths

Whenever students start to feel overwhelmed and slightly panicked, they can stop, tuck their head down, close their eyes, and take five

> Even when students are taking standardized tests for which timing is tight, it's better not to answer one or two questions because of time constraints than to answer the majority wrong due to panic.

deep breaths to regain focus (without disturbing their classmates or teacher). It only takes thirty to sixty seconds, and helps them regain focus so they can continue the test with more clarity. Even when students are taking standardized tests for which timing is tight, it's better not to answer one or two questions because of time constraints than to answer the majority wrong due to panic.

Take a Break

When taking a test, sometimes students get overwhelmed in their seats and work themselves into a frenzy. In that case, students can regroup by getting up to sharpen their pencil or to go to the bathroom. This is a last-resort technique, but it can work well as long as the teacher allows it.

If your son is struggling with testing anxiety, making the school counselor or teacher aware can be incredibly beneficial, because he or she may have some classroom-based strategies or alternatives that could help your son work through his anxieties. Talking to an outside counselor or therapist might also be helpful for developing coping strategies and working through specific fears.

FAQ: MULTIPLE-CHOICE TESTS

1. My son struggles with Scantron and/or multiple choice testing. Do you have any suggestions?

Students struggle with multiple-choice tests for different reasons. Some look at the answers and feel convinced that any answer could be right, depending on the way you look at the question. An easy solution that works for many students is to have them cover up the answer choices and look only at the question. Based on the question, he thinks about what the answer should be before even looking at the answer choices. That way, he is able to think for himself before looking at the possible choices and getting confused.

Scantron tests are similar to standardized tests, with little bubbles to fill in. Some students have challenges with the Scantron answer forms themselves. If you think that might be the case (for example, he becomes overwhelmed by looking at the bubbles and trying to line them up, he can't fill in the circles neatly and completely, or he has a learning difference that makes the letters hard to distinguish), he might see if his teacher would be willing to let him try writing his answers in a test booklet; if his score is significantly higher, this approach should be seriously considered for all his testing, if allowed.

On Scantron and multiple choice tests, I encourage students to never spend too much time on any one question. After giving themselves a good thirty seconds to see if they can figure something out, they should make a small mark by the problem number and come back to it when they are done with the entire test.

Long-Term Projects

Tina, a parent whose children I've worked with, was rightfully exasperated after spending a Sunday afternoon driving to one of her son's classmate's homes for a group project. The students had almost a month to work on the project, but they had left it for the last minute. As a result, she was stuck in traffic for nearly ninety minutes on Highway 101, and her son's group was not even close to being done with their project. As an eighth grader at a nearby private school, he clearly had not figured out who lived where before choosing with whom to work on this project. He could have been busily completing his project with classmates who lived two streets over instead of spending a good chunk of Sunday afternoon on the highway while thousands of other drivers were trying to get to a San Francisco 49ers game.

I have some tips for how to avoid Tina's fate.

Think Before Joining

If it's a group project, advise your son to think before joining a group. I know that the notion of group projects is a great one—teamwork, learning to work with people with different working styles (just like the real world!). The truth is, and we all know it, group projects can be a pain, especially if they require students to get together outside of school hours. Students often have such different schedules that coordinating meeting times and locations can be a hassle. Sometimes groups are assigned, and there is no choice, but after her headache on the highway, Tina talked to her son, Sean, about choosing his group mates wisely, not only on the basis of whom he worked well with and who would get the work done but also whose home might be most convenient. *Note:* Younger kids can be really bad at scheduling and setting times to work. With students in middle school, you might need to call the other parents involved so that you can gently get the ball rolling.

Encourage Your Son to Use His Outside Interests

Whenever possible, encourage your son to use his outside interests to make long-term projects more rewarding. Long-term projects tend to be extensive and can even become grueling, especially if they are on a topic about which your son is less than enthralled. By tying a project into one of your son's outside interests, he will likely become more actively engaged and be more invested in the project being successful. For instance, Sean loves making movies, so his group chose to make a movie about the historical time period they were working on in history class. One of the other students in the group wrote the script, and three of the other group members acted out the scenes, while Sean got to take his turn at directing and editing the film.

Think Big Picture, Then Small Picture

Once your son has chosen what he is going to work on for his long-term project, have him break the project down into simple, small manageable tasks. On a blank sheet of paper, have him list everything—right down to the very smallest and simplest of tasks. If he is working in a group, the team can later work to delegate each task. Then, have him create a timeline for accomplishing the tasks, and after that he should write each of the smaller tasks on his planner as though it were a real assignment because each is a legitimate task for his daily block of homework time. This is not a natural or easy job for most kids to do, but stress and anxiety seem to dissipate once they spend fifteen minutes mapping out how they are going to complete a long-term assignment. Have your son put a box next to each task, so that once it is done, it can be checked off (which can be very gratifying!).

Be a Background Singer, Not the Lead Vocals

I often see well-meaning parents get overly involved in long-term projects, as though their junior high school and high school assignments were such cherished memories that they are dying to redo them. Don't. Offer background support as needed, but let your son figure out the details on his own so that he can be accountable for his own project and reap the rewards of his own efforts. For instance, when one of my students was working on a bridge for his high school physics class, he discovered he didn't have enough hands because his

Offer background support as needed, but let your son figure out the details on his own so that he can be accountable for his own project and reap the rewards of his own efforts.

partner was at a swim meet all weekend. He had his mom and younger sister help him with gluing together parts of the project, but the design, implementation, and direction were all his. In fact, his mom later laughed at how impressed she was by his leadership skills, and that she could see him managing a small company someday.

Writing Essays

As any English teacher will tell you, there is no right way to write an essay. Because essay writing can be so amorphous, boys are often at a loss for how to begin. Typically, they start staring at a blank computer screen around 8:00 the night before the five-page essay is due and then start rambling—off topic, on topic, and then off again. After widening the margins and increasing the font size, they finally get to five pages. It's a painful process for the student, and I imagine an even more painful process for the teacher who reads through those last-minute, multi-topic, eccentrically spaced creations.

Lindsay Holland, a writer and English teacher who works at a nearby high school, helped me develop my method of working with students on expository English essays. I developed a rough outline that I give my students every time they need to write an essay. It's based on the claim, lead-in, data, warrant method of writing essays; if your child's English teacher is opposed to that style, you should create your own outline using the format the teacher prefers, using the outline on pages 157–158 as a guide.

Kids *love* the essay outline and often ask me for blank copies when they have an upcoming written assignment, because instead of having to stare at a blank computer screen, they just need to fill in the blanks incrementally, and before they know it, they have an argument, supported by data, and an explanation for those data. This process helps them to see the logical flow of the essay where they once were finding themselves at a loss, and they start to become more confident in their abilities to organize their own thoughts and ideas.

The following sections detail some important points.

NOTE: If your child's teacher has a different method or structure that he or she wants students to use, you can adapt and create an essay outline sheet accordingly. Sometimes, teachers give specific structural advice for compare-and-contrast essays or other written work. The key is for students to *brainstorm effectively before sitting down to a blank computer screen.*

Active Reading Saves Time

Writing in the margins, underlining important points, and making notes on the characters while reading can all help your child spend less time searching endlessly for that "one line!" that he needs to find in the three-hundred-page book. When he starts to read assigned material, encourage him to make a note every time he sees one or two themes come up in the novel—for example, in F. Scott Fitzgerald's *Great Gatsby*, he could make a note every time he reads something having to do with the idea of love or money. A theme can just be an idea or value—some kids become intimidated by the word *theme*, but it could just be related to the idea of compassion or justice or social isolation. Noting the theme whenever it appears can keep him actively engaged while reading the book and can also set him up for writing an essay later.

The Biggest Questions

After he finishes the book, ask your son to write down the five to ten biggest questions he had about the story. Most times, when a student is asked to come up with a thesis statement (or main idea) point-blank, he shudders and retreats. Instead, encourage him to sit down with a blank piece of paper and write down five or ten questions. This exercise encourages him to think about the book and consider what interests him and what he would be most inclined to use as a topic. After all, writing about something that interests him will make the process more engaging. After he has written the questions, ask him to think about what themes he finds within those questions. As he creates questions, have him ask, Why? For example, if your son is struggling with an essay on, say, *Catcher in the Rye*, you could ask him why Holden Caulfield hates phonies so much, or why he is so upset when his teacher caresses his hair. Questions like these point to the universal truths in the book and might also produce a strong reaction from an adolescent boy.

> After all, writing about something that interests him will make the process more engaging.

The Bubble Chart

Encourage your student to use a bubble chart to help him visualize and make connections. Using a character, main theme, or idea (love, power, money) as a main bubble, have your son brainstorm other ideas off of that one character or idea that he wants to explore further. Allowing him to brainstorm and explore in a free-flowing way encourages an active thought process and helps him become more engaged in his own writing so the assignment doesn't feel like a boring chore.

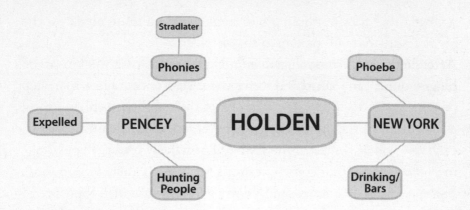

A Controversial Argument

After brainstorming, your child should now develop a controversial argument and make it universal. A controversial argument is one that could be successfully argued both ways. Encourage your son to come up with this type of statement and then take a stand by defending one side of the argument. Whenever students have a difficult time understanding this idea, I use an example from their own lives: "Kids who have cleaner rooms get better grades." Controversial, and both sides could be argued. Another possibility is, "The more involved a parent is, the better the child's grades." They'll love that one.

Incremental Chunks

Encourage your son to break down the essay-writing process into incremental chunks. By working ahead and using the two-hour blocks to complete parts of the essay incrementally, he will have the time to tackle the assignment in smaller, more manageable pieces; thus, he will not be overwhelmed by the prospect of writing a complete paper. Many wonderful English teachers prepare their students for writing an essay by assigning smaller writing exercises along the way that build up to the larger whole. Unfortunately, some students fail to see the bigger picture, scribbling brief answers with little thought, not realizing that they're missing out on a crucial building block for the bigger essay that will be due in two weeks.

Other times, a teacher will simply give students a week to write an essay, plain and simple. If that's the case, I encourage a four-step process that reduces stress and improves their ability to create a solid essay. Although the process is divided over four days, the time spent on each step will be shorter if the student has actively read the book (taking notes and writing some questions for himself), has a good sense of the plot and characters, and knows what his intended topic is.

Here are the steps:

Day 1: Work on the thesis and two to three supporting points.

Day 2: Fill out the outline (see pages 157–158) or fill out an outline in the format your child's teacher prefers. Work on finding all the data points (or quotes) from the book to back up the argument or points being made.

Day 3: Write a first draft on the computer.

Day 4: Edit and revise the draft on the computer. Print out a copy and read it aloud to catch grammatical errors. Look for typos, spelling errors, and other mistakes. Print out the final copy. *Put the completed essay in the appropriate binder.*

Review

Students should make sure to write the essay early enough so there's time to review. Having even a day between writing the rough draft and editing for the final draft can make a big difference. Many times, when a student sits down and looks at what he created a mere twenty-four hours before, he is able to view things with fresh eyes and immediately spot errors and mistakes. The goal is to have students start to see their own mistakes, rather than having the essays heavily edited for them by a parent, tutor, or teacher. I encourage students to read their essays aloud because they can usually catch something that doesn't sound right or is missing a word or phrase. Because the goal is for them to become resilient and self-sufficient, creating the opportunity for them to be their own editor *first*, before relying on outside help, is the key for them to improve their writing skills.

The goal is to have students start to see their own mistakes, rather than having essays heavily edited for them by a parent, tutor, or teacher.

Studying for Finals

Finals do not need to provoke anxiety or hair pulling. One of the most important things to remember about finals prep, as with all other studying, is that active studying is more productive than passive studying. With active techniques, the week of finals becomes much less stressful and is essentially one big week of flipping flash cards, allowing your son to get plenty of sleep and feel rested and ready. I find that students who follow the schedule outlined here report that they got through finals feeling more in control, less stressed, and more satisfied with how they performed.

To successfully prepare for final exams, students should take the advice given in the following sections.

Create Study Packets

About a week before finals, have your son create one eleven-by-fourteen-inch clasp manila envelope for each class. Have him write the name of each class on the outside of the envelope and then put everything that he needs to study for each final into the correct envelope. The envelopes will contain, for example, the final review sheet, answers, old tests and quizzes, important notes, and flash cards (clipped or rubber banded together so they don't get out of order or fall out). The envelope should include everything (besides the textbook) the student needs to study for the test.

Making study packets really helps students lower their anxiety, because it allows them to pull out what they need from their binder to prepare for their finals and not feel overwhelmed with tons of irrelevant information. Instead of looking at a huge stack of materials, they pare down what they need into a single manageable packet that is self-contained and easily transportable.

TIP: If your son's teacher conducts binder checks and administers a grade for them, by all means have him create the envelopes *after* the binder check!

Start the Week Before Finals

The week before finals is the time for heavy lifting. Most students incorrectly assume that the week of finals is the intense time for getting prepared. About a week *before* finals, students should add another two-hour block to their homework time each evening and devote it to getting ready for finals, working on final review sheets, going over old tests, creating their own review sheets, and making flash cards. During the week *before* finals (not the week *of* finals) studying should be intense. Most teachers distribute their final review sheets early, and many schools now implement a dead week before finals, when no new assignments can be given. Ideally, all review sheets and flash cards are completely prepared two days before final exams begin, so that the last days can be spent mastering the material.

Help Him Schedule His Time

Block out time for studying and for stress relief. On page 159, I provide a sample study schedule to help students manage their time. For each two-hour study block for finals, I generally have students choose two subjects, one easier subject and one more difficult one. Why? For many students, it is tough to study any one subject for two hours straight, and it is often easier to toggle between subjects, especially if one requires a bit less intensity. You should notice on the study schedule that there is time between each studying block of an

> For many students, it is tough to study any one subject for two hours straight, and it is often easier to toggle between subjects, especially if one requires a bit less intensity.

hour or two. During that time, students can do whatever they want; it's a great time to work out, take a walk, or do something else to burn off stress and take a break.

Final Thoughts

These methods have worked wonders in helping students transform their academic performance and feel more confident. The most important piece is obviously how it is presented to them (incrementally, in bite-size chunks and with the right approach); the classic win–win. It may seem impossible to try to encourage your son to adopt these habits, but I have seen it done countless times with kids whose parents were doubtful.

Summary

There are few things in your child's academic life more stressful than tests and large projects, and one surefire way to make these tasks more stressful is to approach them in a disorganized and last-minute manner. Having an advance plan for dealing with tests and projects not only decreases anxiety but also, in my experience, results in better learning. Here are some ideas:

- *Test and quizzes:* Remember, studying for tests and quizzes is similar to everyday academic work. Schedule the time, include breaks, and give your child the best techniques for the job. Flash cards are indispensable because they promote an active learning model as opposed to rote memorization. Be aware of the signs of testing anxiety and know what you can do to minimize it.

- *Projects:* For long-term projects, take the time to ensure that your child has a realistic plan for getting the work done and try to take a supporting role rather than an active one.

- *Essays:* All most kids need is a way into the material and a logical structure to follow, and they'll be able to turn out well-conceived essays with minimum stress (see the "Essay Outline Worksheet" on pages 157–158).

- *Final Exams:* If your child can put together a good study packet (which most teachers are eager to provide) and set up the right study schedule, final exams need not be any more stressful than any other part of academic life.

■ ESSAY OUTLINE WORKSHEET

Introduction

- Thesis: Mention three supporting points in the last sentence of the introduction.

Paragraph 1

- Claim 1: One sentence that goes further to argue one of your supporting points.
- Lead-in: Introduces the quote and/or evidence, tells the reader the evidence.
- Data: Quote or evidence.
- Warrant: Two to three sentences showing why you chose this piece of evidence, how it supports your claim, and how it further supports your thesis.

Paragraph 2

- Claim 2: One sentence that goes further to argue one of your supporting points.
- Lead-in: Introduces the quote and/or evidence, tells the reader the evidence.
- Data: Quote or evidence.
- Warrant: Two to three sentences showing why you chose this piece of evidence, how it supports your claim, and how it further supports your thesis.

Paragraph 3

- Claim 3: One sentence that goes further to argue one of your supporting points.
- Lead-in: Introduces the quote and/or evidence, tells the reader the evidence.
- Data: Quote or evidence.
- Warrant: Two to three sentences showing why you chose this piece

of evidence, how it supports your claim, and how it further supports your thesis.

Conclusion

· Reaffirms your thesis and the main points of your argument.

GENERAL WRITING TIPS

• **Write in the present tense.**

• **Avoid the passive voice. (Grades are given to us by the teacher.) Try to use the present tense instead. (The teacher gives us grades.)**

• **Avoid the phrases *this is* and *that is,* instead choose specific subjects and active verbs.**

• **Use commas and conjoining words (and, but, although) to make sentences more complex.**

• **Avoid using multiple prepositions (with, of, about) in one sentence.**

• **Avoid using first person (I, you) unless it is a personal essay or narrative.**

■ SAMPLE STUDY SCHEDULE FOR FINALS

December	Sunday 5	Monday 6	Tuesday 7	Wednesday 8	Thursday 9	Friday 10	Saturday 11
Morning		School	School	School	School	French Chemistry	English History
Afternoon		School	School	School	School	History Math	Chemistry French
Evening		Chemistry French	History English	Math Chemistry	English French		
Finals Week	**12**	**13**	**14**	**15**	**16**	**17**	**18**
Morning	Chemistry final	French final	English final	History final	Math final		
Afternoon	Math English	History	Math	Math			
Evening	French	English	History	Math			

STUDY GUIDELINES

- The week before final exams, pull together all the materials you need to study (including review sheets, old tests, and notes).
- Each night, spend time outside your normal two-hour homework time filling in all the review sheets.
- Fill out all the review sheets and make flash cards by December 12.

Healthy Mind, Healthy Body

Helping Your Son De-Stress, Recharge, and Grow

One of the most important things parents can do for their son is create and foster a healthy environment. By this I mean both an emotionally supportive structure within which he is free to explore and be in charge of his own destiny and a physically robust routine by which his body and mind can thrive. During the middle school and high school years, boys are developing physically and emotionally. And with changes in their physical appearances, hormone shifts, and the environmental stressors of school, friends, and family, it can be a time of intense pressure. Add an unhealthy environment to that picture, and you can see that even the most dedicated boy will find it tough—if not impossible—to practice the time-management and organizational techniques we've discussed so far.

Don't worry, a healthy environment can actually mean *less* work, and a simpler lifestyle, than the routines you're probably trying to stick to right now. Just think how many times illness caused the best-laid plans to fall apart or how often your sleepy and/or exhausted son missed out on something special because he just didn't have the energy (or perhaps the motivation) to take on a new opportunity. Healthy environments foster healthy kids with healthy appetites for new challenges.

Healthy environments foster healthy kids with healthy appetites for new challenges.

In this chapter we'll look at five basic areas in which choosing simpler, healthier alternatives can make a huge difference in a boy's emotional and physical well-being.

Diet and Nutrition

When boys come into my office after school or sports practice, they are typically famished and feeling lethargic. More often than not, they're suffering a low-blood-sugar hangover from the high-fructose caffeine drink that gave them that quick sugar rush before practice. I remember one sophomore boy who came into the office after track practice with a pint of ice cream. He was a half hour early for his appointment, so he sat in the waiting room and devoured the entire carton. By the time he made it into my office, he complained of a stomachache, and midway through our appointment, he looked like he was about to fall asleep.

In my work, I talk with boys briefly about nutrition because I truly believe that it's part of a network of integral factors that affects a student's ability to learn, process, and develop. Research has shown that common nutritional slip-ups such as skipping meals, skimping on breakfast, and not getting enough iron can have measurably negative consequences for learning. Whenever I talk with parents about nutrition, they admit that they feel like there is not much they can do and that there are unhealthy choices everywhere for their son to eat. Some moms complain to me that even if they send their son with a lunch to school, he ends up buying cafeteria snacks processed with chemicals that are illegal for consumption in other countries. But the truth is, parents can make simple changes to create a difference in the choices their sons make in terms of healthy habits.

Create Opportunities for an Easy Breakfast

Jodi Greebel is a Manhattan-based nutritionist and founder of Citrition. She frequently works with middle school and teenage boys and says that one of the biggest issues she sees is that they are not eating breakfast. Many boys prefer those precious few extra minutes of sleep and wake up too late to be able to sit down at the table and eat breakfast before school, which would be ideal. Some boys (and adults) have gotten so used to skipping breakfast that they're convinced they *can't* eat in the morning. But, breakfast really *is* the most important meal of the day. It's very difficult for a growing boy to think straight, concentrate, and focus on his math test if he hasn't eaten since 8:00 the night before.

> It's very difficult for a growing boy to think straight, concentrate, and focus on his math test if he hasn't eaten since 8:00 the night before.

Though sitting at the table and eating for even five or ten minutes is ideal, if your son has trouble finding the time or motivation to eat in the morning, there are many ways to create easy breakfast solutions. Oatmeal breakfast bars or on-the-go breakfast options may be easier for him to carry with him or eat in the car or on the walk to school (again, not ideal, but better than not eating at all).

Create a Win–Win School Lunch Scenario

Some parents complain that despite their best intentions, their son won't eat the lunch they send him with and insists on buying his lunch from school, which is expensive and, depending on your son's school cafeteria, can be nutritionally dubious. For middle school and high school boys, I often frame my argument for bringing lunch from home in economic terms. For instance, Paul's mom gave him $25 a week to buy lunch in the school cafeteria, and it was his job to budget his money for the week. He complained to me that he always ran out of money by Thursday, and so he ended up being forced to bring his lunch from home on Friday. He did, however, admit that there were ample supplies from which to create a good brown bag lunch in his kitchen.

Instead of commiserating, I said, "Wow, Paul, you get twenty-five dollars a week. What happens if you don't spend that money on lunch at school?"

He thought for a minute, and said, "My mom said it's my money to budget as I please."

Essentially the money was his allowance, which he was spending excessively on cafeteria food and candy. So, we did the math and figured out that Paul was spending close to $900 a year on school lunches—which he admitted weren't very good—and that if he brown-bagged it, that money would be his to save. His options for packing a brown bag lunch were likely healthier, and he wouldn't have to stand in line at the cafeteria, so he would have more time to sit down with his friends and relax.

Over the next few weeks, Paul started bringing more of his lunch from home, which was not the cool thing to do, but the pull of $900 kept him motivated. He would sometimes buy a snack or dessert at the cafeteria, but for the most part, he brought his lunch from home and packed it himself with two sandwiches, some fruit, and baked potato chips. And it isn't surprising that once he explained the $900 savings to his friends, some of them started bringing their lunches from home, too!

TIP: Talk with your kids about what they would like to see in their brown bag lunch and have them make a list of options they would eat regularly. Be sure to include those items on your weekly grocery list. Set up a quick assembly-line process so creating a brown bag lunch takes no more than five minutes. If possible, have your son pack his lunch the night before. Kids are not going to take the time to put together something they won't eat, but they might not eat what you put together for them.

Make Snack Options Healthy and Tempting

When boys get home from school or from their after-school activities, they are often ravenous. Many schools have lunch early in the day—at 11:00 or so—and by the time these boys walk through the door at home, they haven't eaten for five or six hours, which can be an eternity for a developing boy's stomach. Many moms say their son's normal ritual is to drop the backpack by the door, head to the refrigerator, open the door, and just stand there to contemplate the wondrous choices presented to them. Often, because they are already starving, these boys will go for sugar-laden, caloric nightmares. Not only will those snacks spoil their dinner but they will also make it difficult later when Johnny is trying to do his science homework or study for a Spanish quiz and his blood sugar has plummeted to disastrous levels.

Jodi Greebel notes how many middle school and high school students love dipping snacks, so tortilla chips and salsa, hummus and carrots, peanut butter and celery sticks, and apples and almond butter are all good options that provide sustainable energy. She finds that boys will eat those regularly if they are readily accessible as options and that this type of snack makes it easier for boys to concentrate when they sit down to work.

A few other quick notes about boys and nutrition:

- *Water is always the best option.* Most so-called energy drinks are little more than sugary water filled with chemicals to give them an electric blue, lime green, or hot pink color not found in nature. Eliminating sports drinks and caffeinated drinks from the house can encourage teens to drink water or even 100 percent fruit juice.

- *Calcium is key.* An alarming amount of research is suggesting that children's bones are much more brittle today than in years past. (I see this in my office; every year, five to ten of my students are in a cast for an extended period of time.) Most people mistakenly believe that dairy products are the only way to get calcium, but almond milk, soy milk, hemp milk, nuts (almonds), broccoli, and dark green leafy vegetables are all great sources. Vanilla-flavored sweetened hemp milk—fairly widely available and full of protein and omega-3s—combined with protein powder actually tastes like a milkshake.

- *The den is not a dining room.* Even if your son is eating his meal by himself after coming home late from practice, make sure he sits at the table for ten to fifteen minutes before rushing off to do his homework or whatever else he needs to get done. Ideally, the television is off, and he can simply concentrate on his food. Enabling him to enjoy and digest his food without distractions will allow him some important transition time, and give him a much-needed break before starting homework or going to an evening activity.

- *Desserts after a meal, rather than as a snack.* Instead of serving cookies or ice cream when the kids come home from school, try offering baked tortilla chips and salsa and save the dessert-type foods for after dinner, when students are likely to be less hungry. Again (somewhat like my mantra about instant messaging), it's not necessary to completely eliminate sweets, but rather save them for the appropriate times.

Exercise and Sleep

On a recent trip to New York, I was riding the elevator with a little boy who looked to be in the fourth or fifth grade and had probably just been picked up from school. I casually asked him how school was that day. He looked at me excitedly and said with a gap-toothed smile, "Great, because it's Wednesday and we have gym on Wednesday."

"Don't you have gym on other days?" I asked a little incredulously, remembering my own days in elementary school, where we had gym pretty much every day.

"No," he replied. "We only have gym on Wednesdays. But at my school I am going to next year, we have gym *every day*." He beamed at me.

"That is obviously the school you want to be going to," I said, before stepping off the elevator, and he smiled knowingly.

We've all heard the statistics: Schools now have less recess and more sedentary time in desks and classrooms, obesity among young people is on the rise, and kids today don't get out in the fresh air like previous generations did. Along with good nutrition, exercise and sleep complete a package that allows kids to concentrate, focus, and feel good. When kids don't get the chance to run around and stretch their legs and release energy, they become sluggish and lethargic, and it makes them less able to pay attention in class. Most important, sleep deficits (discussed below) make it impossible for boys to work at their peak inside and outside the classroom, and the lack of sleep has been attributed to increases in depression and obesity.

School and Non-School Athletics and Fitness

I am a big believer that anyone and everyone, regardless of size, coordination, or skill level, should be able to participate in some sort of organized athletics or fitness on a regular basis. Ideally, this exercise would be outdoors, but consistency is more important than location. These days, with recess and outdoor recreational activities being cut back significantly during the school day, boys are especially in need of a steady outlet if they are expected to be able to focus and concentrate. Too many kids are forced to sit still for too long every day at school, and then come home to have to do hours of homework. For a junior high or high school boy who has energy to burn, this sedentary lifestyle can be torturous.

> These days, with recess and outdoor recreational activities being cut back significantly during the school day, boys are especially in need of a steady outlet if they are expected to be able to focus and concentrate.

Midway through his junior year, Shawn was lost. A shoulder injury had left him unable to play football, which he loved, and he was struggling in school. He was terribly disorganized, and his shoulder surgery had made him miss twenty days of school during his first semester, which set him behind because he missed a lot of foundational material, which made it difficult to begin his second semester with a fresh start. When he came into my office for the first time, he seemed dejected.

"I lost my sport," he lamented. "I miss playing so much." He had started going to the gym, where he would get on the treadmill or bike before lifting weights, but his parents threatened to take that privilege away because his grades were so poor. His parents were trying to send the message that school comes first, but this was absolutely the worst way to do it. As Shawn readily expressed, going to the gym was his way of letting off steam. The threat of losing that healthy outlet and endorphin booster made Shawn even more anxious and upset.

Sensing how much he loved his gym time, we created a schedule where it was regularly a part of his routine; he went there—after he did his homework block—Mondays, Wednesdays, and Fridays and both weekend days. That made his parents happy and gave him an incentive to sit down and get his work done.

There Is a Form of Exercise for Everyone

Some kids are not naturally athletic or simply don't enjoy competitive sports, and that is completely fine. But every kid needs to have some sort of regular energy release, and because most kids don't get the same opportunities to run around on the playground as kids did thirty years ago, it needs to be built in to their regular weekly activities. For many of my students, something athletic or fitness-related is one of their personal goals, and I have seen it range from "Run for twenty minutes four times a week" to "Earn a purple belt in karate" and everywhere in between. I am not even opposed to video-game type fitness activities (though it wouldn't be my first choice) if it gets an otherwise sedentary kid *moving*.

TIP: Create a little healthy competition in your household whenever someone watches television so that kids are not just sitting there listless. Every time someone watches a sitcom, create a structure where they have to do a certain number of sit-ups and push-ups or lunges. You can determine how to structure the competition, and it is likely to be more successful if everyone is encouraged to participate.

Recreational Athletics: A Great Option, Not a Consolation Prize

Leonard played on the freshman and junior varsity basketball teams at his high school but then decided he didn't want to make the year-round, traveling-team commitment required for playing on the high school varsity team. In short, the increased expectations took much of the fun out of the sport for him. Instead, he and three of his friends decided to join the local recreation league, where he had two practices a week and one game on weekends. Problem solved.

Not everyone has to play school sports, and unfortunately, in many cases, not everyone *can* play school sports, especially at athletically competitive schools. If that's the case for your son, encourage him to create what Denise Clark Pope, Stanford researcher and author of *Doing School*, calls a "Garage Band Option" (because not everyone can be in the orchestra). Often, perception by peers (and other parents) prevents kids from wanting to play the sport they truly love at a recreational level, but being part of a team can be a great community builder and make kids feel that they are part of something, regardless of the commitment level.

Make Sure It's a Pressure Releaser, Not a Pressure Creator

Junior high and high school sports these days can be intense; competition and dedication levels are at heights parents and grandparents never experienced when they were kids. Depending on the school and the sport, kids can expect up to three hours of after-school practice every day, making some thirteen-year-olds easily put in a twelve-hour day before dinner. I see many school-aged athletes going to early morning or late night practices and traveling across the state (or sometimes even across the country) on weekends for tournaments and showcases before trying to catch up with everything else on Sunday night.

Most kids feel enough pressure from within themselves that parental over-involvement is one of the fastest ways for a sport that was supposed to be a stress releaser to become a stress creator. As parents, your attitude and approach toward their athletic abilities can either be confidence building or confidence breaking. Your son can see your disappointment if he doesn't make the school team or play well in his club showcase tournament. Are most of your conversations about the team and its performance? Do you scream from the sidelines? Do you get visibly upset after a loss? What would happen to you if your son no longer played on the team? When a sport becomes stressful, all of that energy that your son diverts to focusing on athletics makes him less able to process his schoolwork and concentrate in class.

> As parents, your attitude and approach toward their athletic abilities can either be confidence building or confidence breaking.

Slash the Sleep Deficit

According to research from the National Sleep Foundation, most growing kids need about nine and a half hours of sleep, and most children today are running at a deficit; the average middle school child is getting only eight hours, and the typical high school student is lucky to get seven and can average as few as six hours.

Samuel was a high school sophomore when he first came into my office, and after working together for a while, I noticed that he always showed up exhausted. He admitted that he rarely went to bed before midnight. He was a basketball player, about six foot one inch tall, who was not getting much playing time on his basketball team, and dreamed of playing in college. But because he was the eighth or ninth man on his junior varsity team, college basketball was not really on the realistic horizon (though it was on his goals sheet every semester!). After one appointment, trying to convince him to get more sleep, I showed him a research study that discussed how adolescent boys who are sleep deprived may not grow to their full height and cannot perform to their full potential.

Something clicked after Samuel read that article, and he made immediate changes (nothing like a full-blown research study to convince a teenage boy with a dream that sleep is actually important). He started to go to bed at 9:30 or 10:00 on most nights and would get extra sleep on weekends. He would set his cell phone alarm for 9:30 p.m. to remind himself to go to sleep (hilarious, but true!). Essentially, by adding two to three hours of nightly sleep, he added anywhere from ten to fifteen hours of sleep to his weekly total. Three years later, this young man is a walk-on member of a Division I basketball team.

> Essentially, by adding two to three hours of nightly sleep, he added anywhere from ten to fifteen hours of sleep to his weekly total.

I am not trying to say that any kid who gets more sleep is going to be playing Division 1 college athletics. There is a lot more to Samuel's story that doesn't need to be documented here, but sleep is vitally important for growing boys. Many of the boys who use the organizational and time-management techniques highlighted earlier in this book have said that one of the aspects they most appreciate about being organized is the fact that they are getting to bed earlier. Even though circadian rhythm studies suggest that a teenage boy is going to stay up later and want to sleep in the next morning, most of these kids are so exhausted that they will go to bed—and fall asleep—when given the opportunity.

Prioritize Sleep

On page 194, you'll find an activity log that you can use with your child to figure out his schedule and to determine if he is over-scheduled. By keeping communication open and using the log he can start to make choices about what activities he wants to keep and what activities he is going to need to put aside temporarily because he can't do it all (at once). I suggest that parents and students put sleep on the schedule first, schoolwork second, and work backward from there. Realistically, if the sleep isn't happening, nothing else is going to be happening well (including growing, brain development, and general well-being).

On weekends (especially for really busy high school juniors and seniors) let them choose one night a week to go out—Friday *or* Saturday—and have them stay in the other night and rest. They don't necessarily have to go to bed early, but they usually end up doing so anyway because they're exhausted. It's not as good as getting the same required amount of sleep each night, but it's better than not getting enough.

Eliminate Technology After a Certain Hour

A couple came into my office to talk about their son's college application process, and broke in to laughter when they shared their recent discovery on why their son was always looking so tired. They had just gotten the family cell phone bill, which was so extensive it came in a box. It turns out their son was regularly trading text messages with his girlfriend until about 2:00 or 3:00 in the morning. Having him put his phone in a technology box every night at 10:00 reduced that problem. Don't eliminate technology too early in the evening because for many kids it is a primary means of social interaction and important unstructured downtime. But when it is cutting into sleep time, something has got to give. Put the phone in its own bed for the night, and your son will, we hope, get more sleep.

> Don't eliminate technology too early in the evening because for many kids it is a primary means of social interaction and important unstructured downtime.

Healthy Motivations Outside the Classroom

As I've mentioned throughout this book, one of the key principles of my work is helping boys gain more control of their time and their future, and creating spaces where they are in charge of their lives, whether that is through setting goals, choosing their activities, or managing their schoolwork. Being involved in something—anything, really—that fosters their engagement and builds enthusiasm within their school or greater community is ideal. For some kids that might be the school band, whereas for others it might be their debate team or mock trial, and for still others it might be their athletic team or their school's drama department. Many students will find multiple places where their different interests are encouraged, nourished, and developed.

But it's not just about the growth that happens during the school year. For many boys, the summer is an excellent time for personal growth and development, where they are able to leave the classroom and do something different. I feel so strongly about this that I don't think I ever have recommended that a student go to summer school if he wasn't required to. It is my belief that after spending so much time in the classroom during the school year, the summer should be about engaging *other* skill sets, developing new interests, and spending time outdoors. Summer is the perfect time for boys to pursue their individual passions, which strengthens their self-confidence, independence, and self-esteem.

> I feel so strongly about this that I don't think I ever have recommended that a student go to summer school if he wasn't required to.

Here are a few ways that your son can take advantage of the free time of summer and build up his confidence and self-worth.

Get a Job

Jake was an incredibly witty high school sophomore who was thoroughly disorganized. He was a Sincere Slacker who always left the house without one or more of the essential things he needed (lunch, athletic uniform, major English essay). He was one of the quieter kids and sometimes lacked social confidence. As we were finishing up for the academic year, I suggested that Jake get a job as a bag boy at the local supermarket. His parents were initially skeptical on how that type of job would be helpful to his personal growth and development, but I persisted, and they eventually agreed.

The grocery store was within biking distance from his home, and Jake rode his bike to work most days. I didn't see him all summer, but when I ran into his mom one day, she mentioned that he was working twenty-five to thirty hours a week. When he walked into my office in late August, he stood *taller*. True, he had probably also grown three inches, but he had also developed that special self-esteem that comes from earning one's own paycheck (even if the check is for minimum wage). His job allowed him to interact with adults of all ages and backgrounds as well as experience working with both friendly and not-so-friendly customers.

During his first session back in my office, he recounted stories of getting yelled at by customers or weird happenings on the candy aisle, and he had a gleam in his eye from being the only one of his friends with a job. For him, as for most boys, getting a paycheck is huge. (Another student proclaimed after getting his first paycheck, "Who is FICA and why is he taking my money?")

Jake's job was his own; he was responsible for being there on time, and they counted on him. When adults asked him questions, he looked them

> Adults sometimes underestimate the wonderful life lessons that are taught through working at a summer job and earning those first few paychecks.

in the eye and gave them answers. When he got his paycheck, he realized it took him thirteen hours of standing on his feet to earn the sneakers he was wearing. Adults sometimes underestimate the wonderful life lessons that are taught through working at a summer job and earning those first few paychecks. The shift in confidence and perspective when boys have responsibility and ownership for their work can be monumental.

> **TIP:** As I often tell parents and students, getting a job at Mom or Dad's company doesn't offer the same independent, empowering experience as getting a job in the service industry and learning how to deal with the good, the bad, and being in the stockroom at 7:30 a.m. because your boss said so. Sometimes parents plead their case ("His dad runs a perfectly good Fortune 100 corporation, why can't Johnny work there?" Or "We have a family construction business that Cameron could work at."), but really, it can be a sheltered experience when a family member has the power to hire, fire, and supervise.

Learn a Trade

In any given school year, I work with several different boys who struggle academically because they become bored in the classroom, but as soon as they have a hands-on project, they are absolute geniuses. One of my former students learned how to rewire an entire house by the age of twelve and another would take small machines apart and put them back together just to figure out how they worked. For each child, it should be all about finding something that he can excel at, his own personal win. Many boys are terrific at creating and building things, and yet our society sends the message that learning a trade is somehow a second-rate job. To be able to learn a trade in preteen or adolescent years can be an incredible confidence booster and give kids a sense of resiliency—the feeling that they themselves can create something on their own is quite powerful.

Where Have All the Lemonade Stands Gone?

When I was six, my paternal grandmother knit constantly. She could finish a baby's sweater in about a day, and when she started a new project, all other tasks fell by the wayside. Looking at her handiwork, I innocently asked her how long it would take her to make knit caps (at the time, we were living in Connecticut, and it was snowing, so knit caps came in handy). She reasoned she could make about three per day without a problem, and I concluded that would give us fifteen knit caps to sell every week (do you like how I put my grandma to work?!). I did the math, figuring we could sell them for $10 a piece in our front yard, and my parents laughed and said they never worried about me figuring out how to make enough money to get by.

Lemonade stands are the perfect breeding ground for the creative entrepreneurial resiliency that so many of today's kids lack because they haven't been given the freedom to take chances. Think about it: dragging the table outside the house, creating the sign, gathering supplies, making the lemonade, selling to customers, counting the money, and splitting the profits—these all require effort, motivation, and a certain willingness to take a chance. What if no one comes? What if you run out of lemonade? Kids today are sometimes so afraid to experience failure that they would rather avoid trying to sell lemonade altogether.

> Kids today are sometimes so afraid to experience failure that they would rather avoid trying to sell lemonade altogether.

Fostering an entrepreneurial spirit in your son is more than just encouraging him to sell something or to make money by offering a service (for example, dog walking or pet sitting). It's showing him how to take chances, problem solve, and come up with creative solutions.

Old-Fashioned Summer Fun

In our competitive world, we sometimes overlook the importance of simple summer pleasures for boys—sleeping in late, hanging out by the neighborhood pool with friends, going to summer camp, and trekking to the nearby beach, lake, or lagoon. For some students, their summers are busier than the school year—which is unfortunate, because summer should ideally be a time for a good amount of rest, relaxation, and rejuvenation. Fun summer camps—with cabins, counselors, and a wide variety of outdoor activities—are still wonderful ways for boys to spend their summer. Through the years, I have also seen many boys benefit from outdoor camping, rafting, and sailing experiences, because they are able to develop their resiliency and leadership abilities in an environment away from their everyday school community.

Being a Mentor Is a Win–Win

Owen was somewhat of a Seriously Struggling Student, with very little academic self-confidence and a good amount of frustration with his academic abilities. His high school had a community service requirement, and when he was in my office one day he complained that he had no idea what he should do. I suggested that he volunteer at a local after-school tutoring center that worked with fourth and fifth graders on their math and reading skills. He started volunteering once a week, spending an hour helping the kids on homework and another hour playing sports with them outside. The kids looked up to him, and he enjoyed the two hours a week he spent there so much that he continued going to the after-school program every Monday throughout the school year. It meant something to Owen that he could be of use and have an impact on these kids' lives and that it really mattered to them when he showed up.

Most boys love to help once they realize their help is actually needed and appreciated, and being a mentor for younger kids can be a rewarding and confidence-building experience. Some of the high school boys I work with volunteer as assistant coaches for the elementary school sports teams, while others volunteer in an after-school program that combines homework and activity time. The experience enables them to step outside their world and look at the needs of others who look up to them. If you think your son might resist a bit if you were to suggest mentoring, say something along the lines of "I heard of this place that could really use your help" or have someone else whose opinion they trust suggest it.

The Lure and Pitfalls of Video Games

In his recent book *Boys Adrift*, the physician and psychologist Leonard Sax devotes an entire chapter to discussing the phenomenon of video games and, more specifically, how he thinks they fit into boys' emotional lives.

The most important reason boys are so drawn to video games, he finds, is that for many of them it's *their only platform for controlling their own destiny*—they control the outcome for the most part, and if they fail, they can simply restart the level until they master it. There's no real downside to failure, and the reward system is finely tuned to be incremental and addictive. In short, there's no incomprehensible information, grumpy teachers, boring textbooks, or unfair coaches in a Nintendo box, just a fantasy world in which your son is the star. With this in mind, it's easy to

> In short, there's no incomprehensible information, grumpy teachers, boring textbooks, or unfair coaches in a Nintendo box, just a fantasy world in which your son is the star.

see how a child can easily spend tens of hours a week immersing himself in such a world.

However, if you take the appropriate care to regulate both the kinds of video games your son plays and the amount of time he invests in them, you can probably avoid some of the pitfalls that concern Sax. The most important thing, in my opinion, is that video games aren't your son's sole arena in which he controls his destiny. All of the activities mentioned earlier provide real-world, physical, and emotional challenges, and success in those endeavors can easily match and supersede a high score or kill ratio in a world solely populated by pixels. I am not saying that he shouldn't have a chance to score virtual touchdowns or explore mythical worlds, but hopefully he's also working behind the counter at the local deli, helping out as a youth mentor, spending time at the neighborhood pool, and/or creating his own small business.

Emotional Balance

Being a preteen or teenager today is tough. For many kids, spoken and unspoken expectations within their community can make it difficult for them to feel that they are in control and doing well. Even kids who from the outside appear to be doing wonderfully are sometimes caught up with feelings of self-doubt, with disappointments and disillusionment with school, friends, and family. Our society does not encourage emotional openness among boys, and unfortunately, boys are much less likely to ask for help and admit that they need help. You don't have to look too hard within your own community or within the media to see that tough, strong guys are seen as the ideal.

Create Emotional Check-Ins

Just as kids have physical check-ups, I think that all preteens and adolescents could benefit from regular emotional check-ins: How is he handling stress or setbacks? Does he feel that he has friends or a community of people with whom he can truly be himself? Perhaps a weekly family dinner or a Sunday morning brunch with Mom or Dad is the way to make a check-in part of a regular routine. If this doesn't sound like it would work in your household, perhaps a family friend or another adult might be a better person for this task. Driving kids places is also a great opportunity for emotional check-ins—many times parents and students feel more comfortable communicating while in the car. The key is that the conversation is not forced and is more of an open-ended conversation rather than a checklist.

> Driving kids places is also a great opportunity for emotional check-ins—many times parents and students feel more comfortable communicating while in the car.

Be Sensitive to Possible Deeper Issues

In some instances, what parents see as a lack of motivation or disorganization can actually be signs of an emotional issue such as depression or anxiety, which is just manifesting as unmotivated and disorganized behavior. In more than a few times at my office, a young man has come in because his parents are concerned or frustrated (or both) about his grades, test scores, and overall performance in school. Once we begin working, I sense there is more going on than just figuring out where to put papers in his binder and how to study without distractions. I'm certainly not saying that every kid who doesn't latch on to my system right away is depressed, but in some instances, parents overlook the very real possibility that their child's challenges in school could be a symptom of emotional struggles.

In a 2006 study on youth risk behavior, more than 25 percent of teenagers felt sad or depressed every day for over two weeks at least once during a one-year period. Some parents might think, Well, *so?* Life's hard. Tough it up. But for many teenagers, breaking up with a first love or feeling as though they had no friends or feeling overwhelmed by school can be catastrophic, partly because they don't have the experience and perspective that many parents and adults have. For them, the here and now is the worst that they have ever seen.

Get Outside Support and Help Early On

Doug was a high school freshman when he first came to our office, and his small stature and tough-guy demeanor were hard to miss. He had struggled in junior high and had been diagnosed with ADD and auditory processing speed issues. His freshman year, he made the varsity cross-country team, got the best report card his parents had seen since grade school, and seemed to be fitting in at his larger high school. Midway through his sophomore year, things started to slide a bit. He would forget assignments, become angry and frustrated, and seemed completely checked out. He started failing several classes, and his parents became upset that Doug was not getting the same results from tutoring now that he had in his freshman year.

Pretty soon, it became evident that Doug's challenges were greater than the typical teenage angst, and I suggested that they take Doug to see an outside counselor or therapist. Doug's mom, who had just spent ten minutes telling me all the challenges she and her husband were having with Doug's behavioral outbursts and academic struggles, replied simply, "I asked Doug if he wants to see someone, and he says no. It has to be his choice, and he decided that he does not want to see someone."

I wasn't surprised. Most middle schoolers and teenagers struggling with emotional challenges do not readily sign up for outside support, because they often don't recognize there's a problem. They also have a

> Most middle schoolers and teenagers struggling with emotional challenges do not readily sign up for outside support because they often don't recognize there's a problem.

preconceived notion of what therapy or counseling looks like, often from their friends, which makes them think that it's a sign of weakness. It took Doug's mom another six months before she insisted that he see someone, and by then things had gotten far worse. Note that once Doug saw a counselor that first time, he went back every week without any question or challenge and admitted that the sessions were helpful and interesting. He worked with his counselor to figure out better coping strategies for dealing with the problems he was facing and felt it was easier to talk with an objective third party than with his family or friends. The difficult part was getting there that first time.

Getting outside support early can be crucial for a kid who's struggling with challenges he might not feel comfortable discussing with his parents. Involving an objective third party can offer a fresh perspective and help boys gain coping strategies for when things seem really tough. By showing them that it really is okay—and actually a sign of strength—to ask for help and support when needed and to give them access to the proper resources, parents create an environment that promotes emotional and mental well-being.

TIP: Dr. Judy Rothenberg, a child psychologist and junior high school counselor, recommends parents set a time frame for kids who want to handle things on their own. If things are not improved by the end of the month, for instance, than seeing a therapist will no longer be an option. If there is still resistance, she encourages the three strikes and you're out policy, by which a student has to go three times and then decide if therapy is helpful. This method avoids the trap of forcing a child to go to therapy, where he spends the whole first session (his one and only) being resistant. It's much harder to be resistant three times. In her twenty-five years in private practice, Rothenberg only had one instance in which a child decided to stop after three sessions—and that child decided to come back a year later and resume working with her.

The Problem of Over-Scheduling

Throughout this book, I discuss the importance of students becoming actively engaged in something that they are passionate about; I believe that is one of the best ways to motivate and create a spark in a young person. Kids who are involved within their school and community tend to have better social networks, be more resilient, and be happier. However, more and more often, I am also seeing junior high and high school students who are burned out, injured, stressed out, or just plain overwhelmed. The reason? Over-scheduling.

> However, more and more often, I am also seeing junior high and high school students who are burned out, injured, stressed out, or just plain overwhelmed.

When middle school and high school boys are over-scheduled, they lack the time and space to develop completely as students and individuals. They are constantly moving from one activity to the next without crucial time to (1) adequately process the information gathered during the first activity, (2) recuperate from the effort it took to perform that activity, and (3) adjust to the environment of the next activity. This constant motion without an adequate downtime creates a focus on survival rather than growth and leaves kids susceptible to the negative effects of sleep deprivation and stress.

As a high school freshman, Charles was always an incredibly pleasant and hardworking kid who wanted to please. In addition to taking all advanced classes, he was playing school and club sports and involved in some outside activities—each of which required a significant time commitment. One evening he came into the office with his mind racing, and he could barely concentrate or relax enough to finish a math problem. It turned out that between homework and early morning sports practices, he hadn't been able to sleep more than five to six hours a night and had recently started turning to high-energy, sugar-laden caffeine drinks to get him through the day. He was twitching and nervous and could not calm down. I realized very quickly that we were not going to get through any math work during our hour together.

Instead, I started talking with him about his week and gave him a piece of paper to list all his commitments and write out what activities he did and when (for a blank copy of this worksheet, see page 194). He quickly realized that between school, sports, and social engagements, he was working a 100-hour week! We then went through his activities and picked out two or three things that were must-haves—activities that he truly enjoyed and gave him an outlet or made him feel more relaxed. For Charles, it was basketball and his school's Fantasy Baseball Team Club that met once a week during lunch. Those were the keepers.

Then came his Sunday evening youth group, which also had an extra Wednesday night meeting that had become a burden, so he decided to stick only with Sundays. He also admitted that his other sport, club volleyball, was not something he looked forward to, and with travel time, practices, away tournaments, and conditioning he was spending ten to twenty hours a week on an activity that he wasn't even enjoying. In the end, he decided to give up club volleyball and later on possibly try out for the school volleyball team, which played in the spring after basketball was over.

He kept most of his other activities, but with the new adjustments to his schedule, Charles was able to get two to three hours more sleep each night over the course of the week. In doing so, he felt more relaxed and more in charge of his schedule and was able to focus on enjoying the activities that he did participate in instead of feeling as though everything were some sort of chore. Having more time also allowed him to naturally become more organized because he had more time to process information and do his homework and prepare for upcoming quizzes and tests without always feeling as if he were operating at half speed.

OVER-SCHEDULING AND FENG SHUI

The root principle of feng shui, notes senior feng shui practitioner Deborah Gee, is that one must have a balance of yin energy (stillness) and yang energy (action). Over-scheduling can actually hinder productivity, learning, and creativity. When a child is over-scheduled, there is an imbalance toward the yang energy of work, and there is not enough yin energy focused on reflection, and rest. As Gee notes, a child or teenager's actual learning diminishes because they do not have time to empty their minds of clutter. Doing nothing leads to something. When kids have the opportunity to do nothing, they are able to reflect, review, and digest—and explore what they are capable of doing. In doing so, much creativity comes out of that "nothing."

Extracurricular Activities Have Changed Since You Were a Kid

As I mentioned in Chapter 7, requirements of today's school and extracurricular activities are far more demanding—more hours of practice, more traveling, more energy and intensity—than they were for previous generations. I often challenge parents to think about what their own schedule was like when they were in junior high and high school. Most parents admit that although they had activities here and there, there was nowhere near the time commitment that many kids are now subjected to. Not only does each individual activity today require a sizable chunk of time, combine several such activities together, and you've got a recipe for a kid who thinks he can do it all and wants to do it all, but just can't. *Nobody* could.

Clay, the Intellectual Conversationalist, spent hours and hours practicing for debate tournaments. He and his teammates practiced the Oxford style of debate, in which he and a partner prepared both sides of a certain debate topic (it is the same topic for the entire year) and traveled locally and regionally to compete against other teams. The debate circuit is intense and demanding, and thorough preparation involves nights and weekends during the school year and entire weeks during the summer. Clay spent at least eight hours each weekend day either preparing for a weekend tournament or competing. Because there was always more work to be done, he generally pushed his schoolwork to the back burner in favor of his beloved debating prep, and his grades suffered accordingly.

Clay was unable to figure out for himself how to prioritize his time—debate always won out over any other activity, and who can blame him? We all are drawn to those activities that interest us, and without a practical plan of attack, it's natural to choose to tackle the interesting stuff first and procrastinate about the rest. Part of what Clay and I did in our work together was to figure out how long his homework would take him, so that once it was completed, he'd still have time for debate prep. It was important to do the homework first, when he had more energy, but it also allowed him to be more open-ended in his debate prep; he didn't have to artificially cut it off in order to do schoolwork.

It's not just sports that require more energy and dedication than when you were in school—think about how much time is spent fundraising for the band, getting the fall drama ready for production, or going to school choir concerts. Think about the breadth and depth of each additional activity that your child is involved in, and encourage him to actively decide what he can and cannot feasibly do before taking on another commitment. If he is already overcommitted, work with him to pare down his schedule to the most enjoyable and essential activities.

TIP: In many instances, one of the main reasons for over-scheduling is the if-I-don't-reinvent-peanut-butter-and-tap-dance-I won't-get-into-college mentality, a frenzy that is unwarranted and detrimental. In reality, college admissions officers want to see students who are well balanced and passionate about something, not students who will arrive on their doorstep burned out.

Playtime, Downtime, and Family Time

Kids (and parents) often mistakenly believe that as long as they can physically pull off a schedule without having to be in two places at once, then they are not over-scheduled. I have parents say things to me like, "Well, it works out perfectly: middle school basketball practice is from three to four-thirty and then club soccer is from five to seven and then the math tutor comes over at eight." I look at that schedule and wince, because that junior high boy has just spent a full day at school and then has four hours of running around before coming home exhausted and wolfing down dinner before trying to sit down to do homework (much less put up with one-on-one tutoring). There is no chance that he is going to be able to remember and retain any of that information, or that any of his work will have a semblance of quality. He will likely just be trying to put the minimum number of scribbles on a page (hoping his teacher doesn't notice the terrible quality of his work) before trying to get in a few moments of instant messaging—his way of relaxing and escaping from the constant motion of his day and evening—before heading off to bed.

Denise Clark Pope, a Stanford lecturer and the co-founder of Challenge Success, talks with students, parents, and school administrators about the PDF model of what kids need: playtime, downtime, and family time. It's easy to understand how a three-year-old needs and gets his PDF: time in the living room playing with blocks, a well-earned nap, and those precious moments on your lap listening to you read a book. Middle school and high school students also need the same sorts of opportunities for playtime, down time, and family time, but it just looks different from when they were younger.

Playtime

Let's start with playtime. Often I will talk to students about their over-scheduled lives, and they confide in me that they would rather not be doing Activity A, but they know how much it means to their mom, dad, grandpa, cousin, sister's boyfriend, family pet. Nick, the Creative Wonder, swam in addition to playing in his band and working on his music. His dad came to most meets, sometimes showed up to watch the end of practices, and always had a running commentary on Nick's performance. Many observers would have probably thought that Nick's dad was being a supportive parent—except that Nick hated swimming and had wanted to quit for two years but was never able to communicate that to his dad. In Nick's case, what his parents and others would have outwardly labeled as playtime actually wasn't— playtime is about doing something enjoyable and rewarding *to the child*.

> In Nick's case, what his parents and others would have outwardly labeled as playtime actually wasn't—playtime is about doing something enjoyable and rewarding *to the child*.

Most parents (who have greater years and more perspective on life than their middle school or high school student) agree that, ideally, a kid's main goal is to be a kid and enjoy his life, not to prove how much he can handle. But often this message doesn't trickle down to the kids themselves, because our society sends the message that the busier you are, the more successful you are. How many times do you hear adults gush about how much they have to do and how many different things they need to get done? Kids hear that message and want to seem like they can do it all, too. They end up hiding the fact that they feel overwhelmed and are merely going from one activity to another with little feeling of joy or excitement.

Kids need to feel they are able to make choices about what they want to spend their limited playtime doing—at a certain age, they are ready, willing, and able to tell you what they do and do not enjoy doing. Parents sometimes don't realize the effect that their influence has on their child in terms of participating in activities and sports, so you have to remember that if your son really doesn't enjoy an activity, like Nick and Charles, it's not play, it's just more of a grind. *Kids need to feel in control of their lives* enough to give up certain activities if they can't manage the time commitment or if they aren't enjoying it. These boys aren't quitters, instead, they're young adults beginning to claim control over their lives.

Downtime

As for downtime, I firmly believe that it's the main casualty of today's over-scheduling of students. Research actually shows that kids today have twelve hours less free time each week than they did in 1981. The too-busy kid can start to feel as if there is no end to the workload—there is never enough time to reenergize, regroup, and have unstructured free time. Each activity takes a certain amount of energy, both physically and mentally, and each *change* in activity requires an adequate transition time, so leaving the odd half hour between activities doesn't really count toward that necessary downtime. Much of what I tell students who are over-scheduled is that they need to figure out what is really important to them, and see what they can let go of in order to create spaces of free time, even if it is just for an hour each day. Often they look at me with a sense of relief, because it's

> Often they look at me with a sense of relief, because it's rare that anyone—a parent, teacher, guidance counselor—has ever told them to try to do less or make sure that they have ample free time.

rare that anyone—a parent, teacher, guidance counselor—has ever told them to try to do less or make sure that they have ample free time.

Family Time

As for family time, one of the most important resources for any teenage boy is the ability to communicate with parents—which many parents readily agree diminishes rapidly during the preteen and adolescent years. As I talked about in Chapter 2, most boys have a different relationship with their father than they may have with their mother, so they might have a difficult time communicating their needs about what works for them and what doesn't to each parent. They also may want to appear to be more in control for one parent than they feel they need to be for another—maybe dad is more understanding and would tell his son to just do what he likes, but mom is really worried about college admissions, or vice versa. Maybe juggling two sports and a musical instrument and two tutors is too much, but mom and grandpa love coming to the games and dad thinks playing a musical instrument builds intelligence and character. Having regular family dinners is one way to create opportunities for natural conversation—even if every night isn't an option, two or three times a week, with a regular Sunday night dinner, can give boys the opportunity to have some regularly scheduled family time. In addition, having a regular one-on-one time—perhaps you and your son go on hikes together once a month, or go to a certain coffee shop that you both like—can give an unforced opportunity for family time and snippets of conversation.

In talking to boys, it's also important for parents to bring up the subject of feeling overloaded and allow their sons to reveal and describe how and if their schedule is working for them. There are many reasons preteens and teenagers are grumpy, irritable, and sullen, and over-scheduling is one of them (not getting a date to the dance, getting a bad haircut, and being ignored by the cute girl in science class could be others).

Kids Have Different Needs for Downtime, Transition Time, and Outside Opportunities

Just as kids have varying needs for rest and recuperation, what is over-scheduled for one kid might be perfectly fine for another. One mom explained how she realized her son—her youngest of three—felt over-scheduled much more easily than his two older sisters. "When Jackie and Candace were younger, they would happily bounce from one activity to the next, and they loved it," she said. "But I quickly realized that Robert would prefer to do, at the maximum, one activity after school each day. One day after picking him up from school, he turned to me and asked if he could just have a few days where he didn't have to go anywhere after school and got to go home and relax."

Similarly, some kids can easily transition from school to after-school activities and then on to homework, whereas others need more space in between and can't just come home and be expected to start homework right away. What works for one kid might not work for another, even within the same family. Robert and his mom figured out what activities he enjoyed, to what degree he wanted to become involved, and made sure that he always had a set amount of unstructured free time—where there were no set plans—each day.

> What works for one kid might not work for another, even within the same family.

Summary

As a parent, you play an essential role in creating and maintaining healthy environments, which in turn foster healthy kids with healthy appetites for new challenges.

- *Diet:* Opt for healthy choices and try to make sure that meals and snacks are regular and calming (and don't forget breakfast).

- *Exercise and sleep:* Not everyone is a varsity athlete, but we all need exercise. Encourage your son to find the right level of activity for himself. Also don't forget your son needs solid sleep time, and that should be a primary factor in putting together a realistic schedule.

- *Healthy motivations outside the classroom:* For successful activities outside school, jobs, trades, even small-scale entrepreneurship has its place, as does mentoring. Basically, get your son to unhook from the video console and to live in a non-virtual world as much as possible.

- *Emotional balance:* Check in, be alert to possible deeper issues, and don't be afraid to get outside help.

- *Don't over-schedule:* Things are different now from when you were young, and it's easier for a kid to get in over his head. Look for ways to de-stress with downtime, space between activities, and a comfortable fit that suits your child.

■ TIME-MANAGEMENT WORKSHEET

Student Name _____

Date _____

In an effort to assess your workload, please complete the following table. Include information about activities you *know* you will do and about activities you *hope* to do.

Activity Category	Activity Description (for next year)	Hours Required per Week (outside class)
Courses		
Math		
Science		
English		
Social studies		
Electives (including world language)		
	Total hours in school	
	Activity Description (for next year)	
Sport(s)		
Music, theater, art		
Hobbies		
Community, family		
Job, work		
Other (tutoring)		
Preferred amount of sleep*		
Volunteer work		
	Total hours in one week	168
	Total time commitment with this schedule	
Total time left for discretionary activities (talking on phone, Internet, visiting friends)		

*Minimum requirement for most high school students = eight hours.

10

Special Considerations

Students with Learning Differences

Over the years, I have worked with many students with diagnosed (and undiagnosed) learning differences, including ADD, ADHD, processing speed issues, executive functioning disorders, nonverbal learning differences, and dyslexia. I prefer the term *learning differences* rather than learning disabilities because I don't believe it is a disability to learn differently. Educational psychologists will often consult with me when assessing a student for learning differences, and school counselors frequently confer with me to determine what classes would be appropriate for a student given his particular learning challenges. As such, I regularly work as part of the team of learning specialists for children with learning differences. Parents, guidance counselors, and psychologists who refer students to work with me know that for these particular students, good organizational and time-management skills are absolutely critical for their success.

The organizational and time-management strategies provided in the preceding chapters are not only appropriate for children with learning differences but are *especially* helpful and can help you and your child create a foundation from which he is able to discover and recognize his own personal potential. For students with learning differences, acquiring solid organization and time-management skills is a critical part of the overall framework for personal and academic success. Although one of the most important aspects of personal growth for any child is the discovery and nurturing of his own particular gifts, this is especially true for students who struggle with diagnosed learning difficulties. It's vital that these students understand how to measure different kinds of success, and that they are able to feel empowered within their school and outside community.

> For students with learning differences, acquiring solid organization and time-management techniques is a critical part of the overall framework for personal and academic success.

Kyle and I worked together throughout his high school career. Although he struggled academically with ADD and processing speed issues, socially he was the type of kid who could light up a room. A naturally gregarious and charming young man, he could talk his way into or out of any situation. He was the type of kid who would spend a Sunday afternoon painting his father's fence and then come home and shoot hoops for three hours with his neighbors in the front yard. He was a great public speaker and a natural leader, and it was easy to see why people were so drawn to his charisma.

He was also having success in the classroom, having raised his grade point average to a consistent 3.0 after we started working together. He was organized, did his homework on time, prepared in advance for tests and quizzes, and went in during his teachers' office hours for extra help.

But because he lived in the often over-achieving Silicon Valley, he was frequently anxious over what he considered to be his comparatively lackluster performance. As more and more of his friends got admitted to top-tier universities, his spirits fell. Despite all of his hard work and his many talents, he was starting to consider himself a failure.

"Are you doing the best you can?" I asked him one day, when he was particularly glum. "Do you feel like you are working up to your personal potential?"

"Yeah," he replied. "But sometimes it just doesn't seem like enough . . ." His voice trailed off and he seemed a little choked up.

I looked him firmly in the eye. "Well, I consider that a success." And then I went on to list all the things he was amazing at: speaking in front of a crowd, putting people at ease, and genuinely being a good friend.

Unfortunately, in junior high and high school, they don't often give extra credit for those gifts, but in life, I am sure Kyle will be duly rewarded. When he applied to college, we did extra research to make sure he applied to schools that had the appropriate accommodations readily accessible. I have no doubt that he will be running a major organization or heading a big company—he is that kind of leader.

The Particular Challenge of Parental Over-Involvement

As I mentioned in Chapter 2, parental over-involvement can be debilitating to any student because it inadvertently sends a message to the child that he cannot successfully learn and accomplish tasks on his own. Parents whose children have learning differences, however, often *need* to do a great deal of advocating—particularly at the elementary and junior high school levels—to make sure their child has the proper accommodations within the school. These parents' early involvement is crucial to ensure their children's success in school. As

However, it's crucial for these children's academic and personal success for them to feel empowered to be proactive and become their own best advocate as soon as possible.

these children get older, parents can understandably have a difficult time letting go, fearing their child will fail. However, it's crucial for these children's academic and personal success for them to feel empowered to be proactive and become their own best advocate as soon as possible.

Several years ago, I worked with a high school sophomore, Alex, and his mother, Melissa. Alex was the youngest of three—both his siblings were strong students. With her other two children, Melissa rarely communicated with teachers and never really looked at their homework, but with Alex it became the only thing they ended up talking—and fighting—about. Alex had always been a Seriously Struggling Student. He was diagnosed with auditory processing speed issues in elementary school and consequently received extended time on tests (which he rarely used) and had a difficult time adopting organizational or time-management techniques. Melissa had gone over just about every homework assignment with him since kindergarten and was in constant contact with his teachers, often sending one- to two-page emails to each teacher several times a week, detailing Alex's personal struggles with each assignment. Most of the teachers gave Alex passing grades, even when his work and effort were sub-par, because they really did not want to deal with Melissa.

Now that he was in high school, Alex was becoming more and more resistant to Melissa's assistance, and Melissa was realizing that she could no longer help him with many of his upper-level requirements because the material was beyond her. Even worse, by creating an environment in which Alex had never done anything academically without a significant amount of help and support, Melissa had prevented him from accepting and meeting any challenges on his own. He had very little motivation to tackle problems himself, and very few tools to use if he did try. Consequently, Alex was floundering, unable to do the work or even to figure out where to begin.

It took quite a bit of time for Melissa to realize that she needed to let Alex do things on his own and to stop checking in with his teachers so often so that Alex had the opportunity to become his own advocate. She was so afraid of failure that several times over the course of the next few years she would become angry at the teachers or me when Alex hadn't performed to her expectations—and what she thought he could have accomplished with her help—instead of allowing Alex to start to see his own capabilities and receive the appropriate credit and consequences for his choices.

I often have families who come into my office because the parent–son dynamic is changing as their child is trying to detach from the overwhelming support that the parent has always given, and the parents are realizing that they can no longer support their son in the ways they had before.

> Even worse, by creating an environment in which Alex had never done anything academically without a significant amount of help and support, Melissa had prevented him from accepting and meeting any challenges on his own.

Micromanagement Is Especially De-Powering

Whenever a child has a comprehension, retention, or processing problem, he can easily feel isolated. Compared to his classmates, he may work harder to receive the same sorts of rewards and accolades that some of his peers readily accumulate (or he may never receive them at all). That feeling of isolation prevents him from fully integrating with his school and community, making it difficult for a boy with learning differences to feel like he is able to easily navigate the academic setting. If a parent (or teacher, counselor, or other important adult) micromanages and hovers, it sends the message to the

> Micromanaging prevents children from rising to the occasion and from becoming their own best advocate.

child that he can't do something on his own, consequently damaging the student's self-image. Think about it from a kid's perspective: If you already feel like you can't do something, being micromanaged only validates your feeling of inability. Micromanaging prevents children from rising to the occasion and from becoming their own best advocate.

From an organizational and time-management perspective, micromanaging also makes children less efficient because they constantly rely on outside validation and support for their schoolwork and preparation. Instead of developing their own systems that work for them, they have to use someone else's—that of the person who is micromanaging them. It also shields them from the realization that *they themselves* have the power to get things done; that they can try out different strategies and find the right solutions for their needs.

Have Cooperative "What If?" Meetings

Students who work with me quickly figure out that I am most interested in helping them find practical solutions that they can adapt and implement into their life. In order to get their buy-in, I make sure the students figure out what accommodations they need to feel successful. I offer suggestions and potential solutions, but ultimately it is the cooperative nature of our work that motivates the student to make changes or implement accommodations.

In middle and high school, children with learning differences often need some level of accommodations within their school environment to make sure they have a fair shot at success. Depending on the child's individual needs and the suggestions from their psycho-educational assessment, those accommodations can be fairly straightforward (extended time on tests) to somewhat complicated (personal note takers). Nancy Ely is a learning specialist at Marin Country Day School, a private school in Marin County, California. Within the school, she works actively with students in grades six through eight to find the appropriate accommodations—those that empower students to become their own best advocate. Accommodations should always be created with the child, Ely says, and are most effective when the child is an equal and active part of the process.

Parents, teachers, school counselors, and learning specialists all need to work together with the child so that they come up with creative solutions that work within the school setting. In some classes, note-taker accommodations might involve getting the notes from the teacher ahead of time, whereas other classes might pair a student up to receive notes from a certain classmate after each class. Some students may be able to take extended-time tests in a separate room at lunch, and other schools may need to make other adjustments. The most successful accommodations are those that are individualized, based on observation, and create suitable strategies based on the appropriate level. Empowering your child to become an active voice in a meeting regarding his accommodations and learning challenges will empower him to vocalize his needs and encourage him to actively work to find solutions that work for him.

> The most successful accommodations are those that are individualized, based on observation, and create suitable strategies based on the appropriate level.

Regroup, Refresh, Refocus

At home, you can also work together with your son to figure out solutions to help him become more engaged in his own learning process. For instance, setting aside thirty minutes every Sunday and Wednesday night to get organized and file any and all papers might be helpful, especially if he has executive functioning challenges. It can also be the time when he checks online and writes down all his assignments in his planner and double-checks to make sure he has no upcoming quizzes, tests, or long-term projects that he forgot, overlooked, or wished would go away. Establishing an extra checkpoint within your home, and enabling your son to feel he has the ability to regroup and refocus on a regular basis will make him less anxious about getting work together and figuring out what he needs to do. Working with him to set up a study schedule or routines will enable him to figure out what works best for him and will enable you to make appropriate adjustments.

Use Outside Support As Needed

When students come into my office, they know that they are there to get organized, figure out strategies that work best for them, and work on areas in which they are struggling in school. One of the reasons students feel comfortable asking me questions or asking for certain concepts to be explained in several different ways, is that there is no dual-relationship. I am not their classmate or sibling or family friend, and if they ask a question they were too embarrassed to ask in class; I am not going to judge them or make them feel stupid for struggling with baseline concepts. Chances are, they are not going to see me any other time other than in the office, and our work together is focused on their particular challenges without flowing over into other parts of their life.

Kids don't want to fail in front of the people they love most, so with increased age it becomes more and more difficult for parents to work with students on issues surrounding schoolwork and organization. Outside support—a tutor, learning specialist, or aide—gives kids the opportunity to appear vulnerable in a way that they may not want to appear in front of their parents, siblings, or friends. I typically see parents who make the mistake of thinking that because they are a great writer and majored in English they can help their child with his

English papers. Particularly for children with learning differences, this setup can instead make a child shut down and feel he is not able to fully express his needs and struggles.

Many schools have options for outside support, and some schools have learning centers that offer one-on-one tutoring; other low-cost and free options may exist within your community and can be found with a little research. Hiring a local college student who is well versed in the subject might be another alternative, depending on where you live. Whatever avenue you choose, make sure that the support is consistent (the person comes on a regular basis, not just right before a test or when your child is in a panic), your child feels completely comfortable asking questions, and that the outside support is working *with him* to find solutions rather than doing the work for him.

> Outside support—a tutor, learning specialist, or aide—gives kids the opportunity to appear vulnerable in a way that they may not want to appear in front of their parents, siblings, or friends.

Gradually Wean Your Child Off Your Support

Educational psychologist Jane McClure has worked with students with learning differences for nearly thirty years. In addition to performing psycho-educational assessments, she often sees high school students whose parents have inadvertently become "exacerbated helicopter parents" and works with the families to help the students make a successful transition to college and adulthood. One technique she frequently uses is to have the child list *everything* that parents, tutors, or other

> One technique she frequently uses is to have the child list *everything* that parents, tutors, or other outside support staff currently do for him that he will be required to do on his own when he moves out and/or leaves for college.

outside support staff currently do for him that he will be required to do on his own when he moves out and/or leaves for college. This list could include waking up in the morning, making lunch, writing down assignments, printing out handouts, or making flash cards for tests (which your child should be doing anyway, but I digress). Then, the child picks two things that he needs to take responsibility for over the next six to eight weeks—for example, waking himself up in the morning and making his lunch.

McClure explains that it is key that the *child* chooses the two tasks, so that he can take ownership of this effort. Parents should do everything they can to ensure their son's success at those tasks (buy a loud alarm clock, for example, or work with their son to create a kitchen routine for easy lunch making), but then it is essential for them to let go and allow their son to experience the natural bumps in the road of adjusting to a new routine. As those two tasks are incorporated into the child's life, he can move forward and pick new tasks to add to his repertoire.

By gradually weaning him off your overpowering or age-inappropriate level of support, you allow him to learn to succeed on his own.

The Psychological Fallout of Learning Difficulties

Students with learning differences often feel demoralized and inadequate compared to their peers. Even though they often understand concepts and have good ideas, students with learning differences can have a difficult time producing the work. Organizing an essay can be nearly impossible for some, and memorizing information for a map test could take ages for others. Often, they will feel like they aced a test and that they knew all the information (and studied so hard!) until they get the test back with less-than-ideal results. These mixed messages can leave them confused and trying to figure out whether they are smart or dumb. They feel smart when they know the material and are engaged in the learning process, but they feel dumb when they get the test back with an unexpectedly low grade. Sometimes students will come into my office thoroughly puzzled by the way a lesson was introduced in class, but then when we go through the concepts in intricate detail and in a step-by-step fashion, they are able to understand the information fully and process relevant material.

Consistent Affirmation from Outside the Nuclear Family

Every child needs to have consistent wins; an activity or group that they enjoy and feel good about and/or a place in which they feel successful. This is especially important for students with learning differences, who usually don't feel successful in the classroom. For many of these students, being in the classroom, completing homework, and taking tests and quizzes are all a constant struggle, so finding something they are good at and enjoy doing is essential. It's much easier to motivate a kid to get through the struggle of school if he has something to look forward to and feel good about, whether that is building model planes, taking tae kwan do, playing a sport or musical instrument, or being part of team or group.

> For many of these students, being in the classroom, completing homework, and taking tests and quizzes are all a constant struggle, so finding something they are good at and enjoy doing is essential.

Kids with nonverbal learning disabilities, for instance, may feel socially isolated and that may make them feel anxious and unable to concentrate—both in the classroom and after school. Feeling isolated can be emotionally devastating and can affect their ability to become organized and manage their time appropriately. For many of these students, it is helpful to participate in groups and find a social network of other kids with similar challenges who can help them receive affirmation from people other than their parents and relatives.

Find and Reflect on Successful Strategies

Some students will consistently struggle in school because the way material is presented in their classes does not particularly suit their individual learning style. Even so, there are ways to implement strategies that will work for them and help them reach their personal potential for that assignment or task. When students first visit my office, we look at what organizational and study strategies they were using previously (if any) and tinker around based on whatever assignments they have coming up. To motivate students who have spent so long struggling in the classroom, it's important to get success as fast as possible. Then they can reflect on how they achieved that success, which encourages them to replicate those techniques.

> To motivate students who have spent so long struggling in the classroom, it's important to get success as fast as possible.

Essentially we just try a particular strategy (many of which are outlined in Chapter 8) and see if it works. If it does, we reflect on that success: How did making the flash cards for this test help you do better on that test than before? How did starting five days before the paper was due allow you to successfully organize your thoughts? Was it less stressful to listen to the novel as an audiobook? In this way, success is demystified; it isn't magic or an accident. They see how it works, and can look forward to achieving similar good results in the future.

Focus on Study Habits and Each Incremental Success

For any student, but again, *especially* a student with learning differences, it's *imperative* to focus on the study habits rather than the test scores and grades. It may be a while before he sees an improvement in marks, especially if there are a lot of stops and starts—that is, periods where everything is going along smoothly, then there is a little setback requiring a fresh start. That is why building in spaces for constant regrouping (say, twice a week as I noted earlier) can help smooth over those times, so that there is less interruption in the natural flow of work. Eventually, through the repetition and consistent reinforcement that comes with having it as a part of his day, students will be able to pick up and incorporate habits into their lives that weren't previously there.

About a year after her son started coming to my office, Mary was still a little frustrated about all the stops and starts. Marcus still struggled in certain classes, and he certainly did not always get his homework in on time, though missing assignments were now few and far between. But then, in the course of her conversation with me, she reflected earnestly, "A year ago I would have been grateful if he was passing all of his classes. Now, he is passing everything and that isn't even a worry in my mind. What a difference."

She realized that Marcus had made incremental improvements in his organizational and study habits that were actually quite significant and had led to improvements in his grades. He still was struggling, and still had a few Cs in classes, but by *focusing on his study habits* he'd made changes. When Mary reflected over the long term, she started to realize how much progress he actually *had* made.

Creating the Right Set of Accommodations

When I work with students, we come up with solutions that will work best given their individual needs. If I told them only what I wanted them to do to become better organized and manage their time, most of them would look at me as if I had horns coming out of my head. At school and at home, working with students to come up with the appropriate learning solutions and accommodations should

> At school and at home, working with students to come up with the appropriate learning solutions and accommodations should really be done *with* the child so that he has an equal part in the process.

really be done *with* the child so that he has an equal part in the process.

I hope your son's school allows students to be part of the meetings that address his learning accommodations and that the meetings are held in such a way that his opinion and voice are readily heard. After all, the purpose of the accommodations is to set the student up for success in school, not the other way around. During these meetings, encourage your son to be his own advocate and work to incorporate some of the organizational and time-management strategies from this book into his accommodations when appropriate. For instance, Tommy was a seventh grader at a local junior high when we started working together. After he worked with me and learned how to organize his binders and use his planner, he incorporated that into his daily routine in his resource class where he spent one class period every day.

Find Strategies at the Level They Are Needed

When working with a school to come up with the appropriate accommodations, try not to do more than what is needed. I liken it to when parents go to the office supply store and buy the most expensive and intricate supplies, thinking that it will make all the difference. In fact, sometimes the most basic and simple accommodations are the most effective. Using the right tools and technology as a resource (instead of a crutch) allows students to set themselves up for success and still be challenged enough to feel a healthy sense of accomplishment when getting their work done.

For instance, language acquisition is tough for students with dyslexia, so using audiobooks can be a complete relief and can dramatically improve comprehension. When I am working with a student who has dyslexia who has to read a novel for class, I often suggest that they annotate their book while listening to the audiobook. That way, they are actively reading and improving their comprehension by being able to hear the information while they read.

Making things more complicated than necessary just creates an extra layer of confusion for the student, who then has more information and requirements to juggle. For instance, if he is granted the accommodation for getting extended time on tests, see what would work best for him given the school's setup—for example, find the best time and place. Ask him what he would envision being most effective and see how that can be accomplished within the appropriate level of accommodations. Maybe getting notes from his friend after class works better for him than getting a copy of the teacher's notes or vice versa. Perhaps using an audio recorder for some classes really works well but for other classes it's not necessary.

For all of these different accommodations, it's important for your child to play an active role in determining what measures will make his life easier and how they can be incorporated into his personal organizational and time-management strategies.

Communicate Frequently

One of my associates works with a high school freshman, Danny, who is on the autism spectrum and attends a local public high school. He is in mainstream classes, though he does have a resource class during the day where he works on homework. He uses a keyboarding device that is strictly for word processing to take notes in class, and needs the structure and routine that is often important for children on the autism spectrum. Danny has made extensive strides in his ability to be organized and manage his time and comes to our office three times a week for extra support. He made it through the entire first semester of his freshman year without any meltdowns, academic or otherwise, which his parents considered to be a tremendous success.

However, midway through his second semester, we found out that Danny was flunking history. He had become diligent about writing down information on his planner and occasionally brought in his history homework, so we were confused. It turned out that Danny's history teacher had changed the format in which she required work to be turned in—she now had students turn in major packets once every two weeks, but had failed to put that information online or tell his parents or us.

Danny, confused by the new system (which required a bulk of material be submitted all at once, instead of being broken down into smaller assignments) became somewhat overwhelmed and shut down because he wasn't able to understand how to work with this new change. Because we weren't aware of it, we couldn't proactively help him figure out a solution. The weekend in which this all came to a head for Danny (when his parents found out that he was failing history and he had to admit he had done some but not all of the history packet work) could have easily been avoided with more active communication.

After the incident, we all—parents, teacher, tutors, guidance counselor—were on an email list to maintain communication on an as-needed basis. Just knowing that we all communicated regularly also eliminated the intricate stories that Danny weaved when he began to feel overwhelmed and helped us work with him to break down significant assignments into manageable tasks.

Divide and Conquer

In Chapter 8, I talk about how breaking down long-term projects into manageable simple tasks is important for most boys so that they can feel less stressed by the prospect of a large, looming assignment. For students with certain learning differences, this idea of divide and conquer is particularly important. Taking a larger assignment—for example, finishing a novel for class over two weeks—and breaking it apart into reading and listening to twenty-five pages each day with the audiobook is much more manageable. Active reading strategies—reading, highlighting, taking notes for five minutes at the end—are helpful and more manageable when done in small chunks rather than all at once.

Students with a non-verbal learning disorder for instance, may have great ideas for an English paper but have a difficult time organizing their thoughts. Using the essay tips worksheet (see pages 157–158) and talking out their ideas with someone could help them organize their thoughts and make the entire process less anxiety provoking. For a student with slower processing or slower fluency, determining what reading needs to be done on his own and where audiobooks need to be used is one way to divide and conquer. For instance, a student could read the one or two handouts from class if it's more efficient for him than using Kurzweil or another technological resource, but then could use audiobooks to read novels or textbook reading if that is available.

> For a student with slower processing or slower fluency, determining what reading needs to be done on his own and where audiobooks need to be used is one way to divide and conquer.

Add Buffers of Extra Time

Whenever students complain about how much longer it takes them to get certain tasks completed compared to their peers, we talk about how every person has certain aspects of life in which they struggle, and other aspects that come easy to them and how finding the balance of both is part of working up to one's personal potential. It's especially helpful if they have something in which they excel—say, sports, music, leadership, art—so they can be reminded of something that they enjoy and that is relatively easy for them.

For students who have certain learning differences, two hours may not be adequate for completing homework each night. It may take them longer to complete certain assignments and prepare for upcoming exams, based on the way they read, how they think logically about information, and how they process information to make meaning. For students with a diagnosis of ADD or ADHD, sitting and concentrating for more than twenty-five minutes at a time might not be possible, especially at the very beginning, so extra buffer time and weekend blocks will probably be necessary to get the same amount of work completed as some of their classmates.

Instead of the two-hour blocks I talk about earlier in the book, some of the high school students with learning differences whom I work with have three-hour blocks, and then on weekends have three two-hour blocks for completing homework and other assignments. For some students, it may be very difficult to convince them to spend that amount of time completing work they consider burdensome, but that is why finding strategies that are successful for them are so vitally important. When a boy with a learning difference finds strategies that lead him to success, it will motivate him to replicate that success, and the extra time may not be as much of an issue.

For instance, a child with executive functioning disorder or ADD/ADHD will often need consistent repetition and lots of restarts, so having a time every night to check binders and planners, organize papers, and get assignments sorted out will probably be an essential part of their daily structure. I find that for many of these kids, a timer is an essential tool. For instance, setting a timer for twenty minutes before your son starts a homework block for him to clean out his binders, recycle necessary papers, make sure all homework is in his planner, and get any necessary materials to the space where he will be doing his homework will help set him up to be able to complete the work with less distractions.

When working, he may need more frequent breaks, so setting up a timer for fifteen or twenty minutes at first, with a set specific task for that period of time, may help him stay focused. If he becomes focused on the task and can see it to completion without a break—say, twenty minutes goes by and he has ten more minutes' worth of work on his math assignment and he wants to barrel through, great. If not, let him take a five-minute break to get up and move around before restarting.

In my office, many students come in early for their appointments because we have a space where they can check their assignments online and get all of their binders organized. We

For instance, a child with executive functioning disorder or ADD/ADHD will often need consistent repetition and lots of restarts, so having a time every night to check binders and planners, organize papers, and get assignments sorted out will probably be an essential part of their daily structure.

have a cupboard (which they have easy access to) where they can get the hole-punch and reinforcements and other materials to make sure all their binders are in order before their appointment. For many students, that built-in fresh start helps decrease their anxiety and become focused.

Create a Class Schedule That Is Stimulating Yet Appropriate

Throughout this book, I talk about the detrimental effects of over-scheduling students and how over-scheduling can really affect a student's ability to absorb, reflect, and process information. Students with certain learning differences can be especially affected by increased workloads, and understanding the work level involved in certain classes, especially in junior high and high school advanced or honors level classes, is important.

When I work with students and parents and start to think about a student's class schedule, I have them recognize the importance of balance. For instance, if a student struggles with processing speed and/ or fluency issues and wants to take several classes that involve a significant amount of dense reading, he may be able to do the work but the homework load may be overwhelming and may not leave him time for outside activities or rest. It's often complicated to find the balance between being challenged and feeling like he is being set up for success. Having to read three hundred pages every week and having multiple weekly essays due is a schedule that may be overwhelming and counterproductive for a student who struggles with reading fluency.

Working with the counselor, learning specialist, and student and using a time-management table (see page 194) can help you and your son determine the appropriate course load for his strengths and challenges. It will also enable your son to use organizational and time-management techniques more effectively because he will be set up with a schedule he can work with, instead of one that is overwhelming.

Focus on Both Strengths and Weaknesses

Charlie is a high school freshman and has dyslexia as well as several other diagnosed learning differences, including executive functioning and memory issues. He has struggled academically and really had low academic self-confidence when he first came to work with us several years ago. His first few months in high school were a struggle; his elementary and junior high experiences had not set him up with a good foundation for study skills and learning strategies appropriate for his needs.

In the office, we worked on getting review sheets done ahead of time, making flash cards, and setting up a schedule to do work in small breaks. He quickly flourished and even started working ahead on his assignments without any prodding from us. Even though homework took him at least double the time it took many of his peers, seeing that the organization and time-management strategies were successful motivated him to continue. By the start of his second semester, he was in a routine and felt like he knew how to be successful in school and manage his homework and tests efficiently.

Charlie's personal win was through sports and friends—he was athletic and well liked among his peers. His mom figured that because he excelled athletically, she should encourage his personal passions. In the spring, he decided to play club lacrosse on a team that practiced forty-five minutes away twice during the school week as well as being part of the freshman baseball team. Pretty soon, Charlie was spending nearly twenty-five hours a week on sports, and he would come into our office exhausted and barely able to concentrate. He no longer had any time to work on school assignments, with which he now struggled. Just as he was starting to see the success that adapting certain organizational and time-management strategies could bring him, his schedule prevented him from continuing in his progress. Within a month, he'd quickly dug himself into a deep hole academically, and he worked the rest of the semester to get back on track.

Individuals typically gravitate toward their strengths, because it's easier to work on something they are good at than to concentrate on an area that needs improvement or extra attention. Students with learning differences are no different from anyone else; why would someone knowingly try to spend extra time focusing on something when he is seeing only incremental results when there's another (more enjoyable) activity where it's easy to get great results? Like Charlie's, your son's results may be small and take time, but the lessons learned from overcoming weaknesses and working through them can be confidence and character building. As parents, you may have to make the tough decisions to encourage your son to work on his struggles as well as his strengths; very few preteen or adolescent boys will willingly give up playing two outside sports because they feel they need to spend time creating flash cards and filling out review sheets.

Appreciate the Teachable Moment

When Danny came into our office after his history assignment fiasco, his head was down and he looked dejected and demoralized. He knew he had done something wrong—he, like most kids, wanted to do well—and I knew that being stern or forceful at that moment and telling him what he did wrong would have been a disaster. He would have completely shut down, not completed the assignment, and become angry and frustrated and nothing would have been accomplished. Instead, we figured out a plan to get him back on track and get everything he needed to do to complete his task. There was no emotion, anger, or frustration on anybody's part, just a sense of, "Okay, this is less than ideal, how do we fix it?" Later that week, we reflected and used the experience as a teachable moment by talking about what happened and what would have been the better choice should a similar situation come up in the future.

> Regardless of how structured or well thought out and implemented organizational and time-management strategies are, there will be bumps and hiccups.

Regardless of how structured or well thought out and implemented organizational and time-management strategies are, there will be bumps and hiccups. Using those blips as retrospective teachable moments instead of emotionally charged incidents can help students make long-term progress as they work to reach their personal potential.

Summary

The strategies described throughout this book are not only appropriate for children with learning differences but are especially useful and can help you and your child create a foundation from which he is able to discover and recognize his own personal potential. Remember:

- Avoid over-involvement; you'll need to advocate effectively, but you'll eventually need to turn control over to your child.

- Be aware of how learning differences can be assuaged, both by your family and by peers. Success for the child with learning differences is measured in many ways, not just by earning better grades, such as the confidence that comes from finding tools that work for him and demystify learning. Pay attention to your child's strengths and weaknesses and seek out those teachable moments when it's clear how he's progressing.

- The right set of accommodations will be key; work with your child's school to make sure he's got the best help he can get and stay supportive. The most successful accommodations are those that are individualized, based on observation. Come up with suitable strategies based on the appropriate level.

11

Special Considerations

Single Parent/Guardian, Separation/Divorce, and Two Households

One of the added pressures of childhood is the loss of control children can feel when their living situation undergoes a transformation or is otherwise in flux. Some of the students I see in my office have complicated living situations, and those living arrangements can often affect the child's ability to become organized and manage his time effectively. Adults don't always grasp the added pressures that complex living situations place on children because it is often the children who nomadically shuffle between households while the adults typically remain in the same place. Some students have parents who have recently separated, others have parents who have long divorced and since remarried, bringing new step-siblings and living arrangements. Still others

> Adults don't always grasp the added pressures that complex living situations place on children, because it is often the children who nomadically shuffle between households while the adults typically remain in the same place.

spend a good portion of their time shuffling between the home of a single working parent and a grandparent, and a few live in homes with foster parents or another guardian.

In each situation, it's important to place a heightened sensitivity on addressing the emotional, physical, and practical challenges as they relate to the overall well-being of the students because typically, adults can unintentionally overlook the effect of household transformation until there is a reason to do so—more missing assignments, lower test scores, an overall drop in GPA, or a gradual disinterest in school.

Household Transitions Can Cause Major Upheaval

A few years back, a father called me, concerned that his son had seemed to be withdrawn and not engaged in school as much as he used to be. The young man was a high school sophomore and had been doing relatively well until the past few weeks, when he stopped turning in homework and flunked a few math quizzes. Because his son's grades were available online, the father had ready access to them and wanted to figure out what was going on.

"Has anything changed in your home life?" I asked.

"Well, things are a little hectic around here," the father admitted. "My wife's mother, who has been sick for some time, just moved in with us. She can no longer take care of herself and is in her final stages. My wife and I couldn't see to put her in someone else's care, much less afford it." The father then went on to describe all the different adjustments he and his wife were making to try to make the transition as smooth as possible.

"Things are incredibly stressful, though," the father admitted. "[His grandmother] really needs full-time care, and we are struggling to provide it adequately. An aide comes for five or six hours a day, but it is still a struggle."

"Where is your son during all of this?"

"He spends most of his time in his room with the door shut—we think he is probably doing his homework, but we're not sure, and now looking at his grades, that has clearly not been what is going on. He says he doesn't feel comfortable doing his homework in the dining room because his grandmother is usually nearby sitting on the couch in the next room. He barely makes it out of his room for dinner. He was always really close to his grandmother as a child, so I'm sure it is tough for him to see her so sick."

Over the course of our conversation, the father started to recognize the emotional difficulties that his son was going through, seeing his beloved grandmother's health deteriorate, and feeling the strain of having a new addition to their household was making it difficult for his son to concentrate. His son's declining interest in his schoolwork was merely a symptom of his greater life stress: the household and life transition involving his grandmother's declining health.

With his newfound perspective, the father changed his focus from his son's missing schoolwork to helping him cope with the psychological and emotional challenges he was experiencing. That evening, the father had a conversation with his son in which he recognized and validated the stress that went along with the household transitions, and they discussed things that could happen to help improve the situation. Just talking about his fears allowed the student to begin to feel more comfortable. They made some adjustments—his son agreed to see the school psychologist a few times to talk about some coping techniques, and the household

> With his newfound perspective, the father changed his focus from his son's missing schoolwork to helping him cope with the psychological and emotional challenges he was experiencing.

made adjustments so that he had a place outside of his room to do homework for a few hours every evening. The young man also decided to work at the library a few times every week to give himself a change of scenery. Though he struggled over the next semester (his grandmother passed away a month after my phone conversation with the father), the young man was better able to make adjustments and feel validated for the emotional challenges he was facing, and his parents were able to understand what was making it so difficult for him to concentrate.

Any sort of household transition is emotionally wrought with challenges—whether or not it involves moving. Having relatives move in or having a parent move out (in the case of a separation or divorce) can create an undeniable stress in the life of a child and can cause him to become distracted, withdrawn, and otherwise preoccupied, making schoolwork of secondary importance. Simply recognizing and addressing the added stress that any sort of household transition can cause to a young person, especially one who already struggles with organization and time management, can enable parents and children to start to create some solutions that will work within their new arrangements.

Separation and Divorce

Even though divorce rates in the United States are no longer on the rise (they peaked in the 1980s), roughly *half* the marriages in this country still end in a split. Although many of these divorces don't involve children, it's very common to have children either caught up in a family going through divorce, or living post-divorce in some form of nontraditional household.

It's worth mentioning that divorce is a very particular kind of challenge for a boy who struggles with organization and time management. Research has shown that children experiencing divorce are much more likely to suffer academically during the painful early stages, before the family has had a chance to reform itself as two separate entities. In Chapter 12, I discuss serious illness and how that can affect even an organized boy; the early process of splitting up a family can have similar effects. This shouldn't come as a surprise because in a sense the family itself has been irreparably injured and each person in the family will need time to adjust to a life that will never be quite the same as before.

When Michael first came to see me, he was a freshman at a local public high school, and his mom was concerned about his organization and time-management skills and about the fact that he seemed withdrawn and uninterested in school. His binders were in disarray, and he used his planner sporadically. When I met Michael, his initially depressed countenance gave way to an animated and amiable young man, as soon as I started asking him what was really going on in his life.

Michael had all sorts of interests, from playing the trumpet to hanging out with his grandparents—who lived down the street from him and who he truly adored—and was genuinely interested in being organized, even though he struggled to find homework assignments and to study for tests. Though I initially thought he did not like his new school, I quickly found that he was well adjusted with a good set of friends and felt part of his high school community.

After our first few sessions, he reluctantly mentioned that his parents were newly separated, and that his father had just moved out. Michael's mom neglected to mention that to me when she first called—mostly, I think, because she was traumatized by the separation and having a difficult time admitting its impact on every facet of their lives. By not mentioning it to me, though, it was as if she did not see the correlation between the major upheaval in her son's life (sister leaving for college, parents getting separated, all within eight months) and the effect that it could have on Michael's ability and desire to stay engaged with his schoolwork and his friends.

As Michael and I started to work together, he set goals for

Emotionally, just being able to admit that the arrangement was difficult seemed cathartic to Michael and enabled us to come up with solutions that would make his life easier when it came to getting his work done.

himself and generally became more organized—he used his binders and planner, and fewer papers ended up at the bottom of his backpack. In the beginning, he spent weekends at his dad's sparsely furnished new apartment, where he did not even have a table where he could do his work. Emotionally, just being able to admit that the arrangement was difficult seemed cathartic to Michael and enabled us to come up with solutions that would make his life easier when it came to getting his work done. What his mom thought was disinterest in his new school was really more of a frustration and grief over the end of his family as he knew it.

We tried several different arrangements and eventually agreed that he would try to get his homework done on Friday afternoons before he went to his dad's and then finish up work when he came back to stay with his mom on Sunday evenings. He admitted that he felt more comfortable at his mom's (she was staying in what was once the family home) and that he did not like going over to his father's new apartment because his dad spent most of the time watching television. But Michael felt that he had to go because that was the arrangement that his parents worked out.

In his sophomore year, Michael got his driver's license, which made it easier for him to shuttle between homes. Having a car to use gave him a sense of control and a place to store all his stuff when he was between homes. He still did most of his homework at his mom's, but would bring his backpack in case there was an opportunity to do work at his dad's; he recognized that there wasn't much to do at his dad's apartment, and he might as well get work done. By this time, his father had purchased a kitchen table, so Michael had a space to do schoolwork in each place if he chose to do so.

One of the biggest issues for Michael and other boys whose fami-

lies are transitioning into two households is that they often have difficulty remembering things when they have more than one house. They
rarely have all of their books with them, and they can't remember in
which house they used the computer and thus which machine stored
the homework that was due that day; can't remember on whose backseat the sports bag, lunch, or permission slip was left on the way to
school; can't remember to ask for money to buy the paperback book
that was supposed to be in class yesterday for English; don't know
where the inhaler is (under the bed at one of the houses?) and allergy
season has just started; and forgot again to make the bed before leaving
for school, which is the rule only at dad's apartment. For many of these
students, the school front office becomes the drop-off center and half-
way house for their books, missing homework, and other supplies.

With Divorce, Focus on the Parenting Plan

There is a general consensus among experts that once a divorce is agreed
upon, a detailed parenting plan is essential. In fact, many states require
a parenting plan as part of the legal custodial settlement before granting
the divorce. These plans can be (and perhaps should be) *extremely* detailed, laying out in specifics how the parents are to work together in the
coming years to help raise their children while living apart.

There are many thoughtful books out there detailing what makes a
good parenting plan—what to include, how to be specific while remaining flexible, common mistakes to avoid—but in my experience few
of them focus on the child's academic needs beyond the basics (which
parent will pay tuition and supply bills and who will attend school
meetings and events). Nowhere in these detailed plans are there specifics about where homework will be done, how study spaces will be set
up, and other crucial details for boys who struggle with organization.

The rest of this chapter discusses in detail the organizational challenges faced by boys who move between two households. For those

For those of you who are in the midst of setting up a plan for sharing custody of children (particularly if you have a son struggling with time management and organization), make sure your parenting plan includes specifics about study times, places, and techniques.

of you who are in the midst of setting up a plan for sharing custody of children (particularly if you have a son struggling with time management and organization), *make sure your parenting plan includes specifics about study times, places, and techniques.* That way, these details become part of both households' overall structures as you move forward and will ensure these important organizational details carry the same weight as other myriad aspects of two-household life. As you'll see, many of the topics I cover (such as transitions between households and communication between the involved adults) are things you're already including in your parenting plan and may require just a bit of tweaking to make them work for your son's organizational needs as well.

Also remember that you and your parenting partner are living examples for your son. He's paying attention to how you two deal with difficulties. If you show him that organization is crucial to facing difficult times as well as part of a normal life routine, it will have a deeper impact. Every family's situation is unique, and some custody arrangements are more complicated than others, but time management and organization can be a tremendous advantage for families undergoing the huge challenges a split will introduce.

> **TIP:** Whatever the new schedule is, it has to include set blocks of time for homework, and the kids have to be able to remember the schedule. When adults start making swaps in the schedule, most kids (who are trying to please both parents) will not tell their parents that the changes drive them crazy or that they can't even remember where they're supposed to go on any given day.

Two-Household Challenges

It can sometimes be difficult for parents to recognize the weight of the additional organizational challenges students face when they spend significant time in two different households. Consistent and uniform approaches and structures are not always possible when the two homes have distinctly different lifestyles (for example, remarried Dad has a new baby while Mom is single, or Mom's and Grandma's ideas of house rules don't exactly mesh), but there are several approaches that parents can work on together to help their sons feel more in control of their shifting surroundings.

When interviewing adults and students for this book, I talked to a lot of families who had, in many respects, succeeded in the delicate and difficult challenge of empowering their son to be independent while also giving him the tools to maintain a semblance of control between two different households. Each of the families differed in terms of how they split time between the two homes and how they arranged details such as sleepovers and soccer tournaments, but all of the families had worked together to create a system that worked for their children and themselves.

Ultimately, each family's situation is unique—some kids I work with spend an equal time at Mom and Dad's, while others spend every other weekend with one parent and with the other parent the rest of the time. Others have grandparents who play a major role in their life and they spend several nights each week there. Still others have designated nights and switch off almost every evening—something I generally would not recommend—and have been doing so, successfully, for years. There is no one right way to do things, by any means, but there are things

> There is no one right way to do things, by any means, but there are things both parents can do to help facilitate easier transitions between households.

both parents can do to help facilitate easier transitions between households.

When I first started working with Jeremy, he seemed a bit apathetic about studying, and one could hardly blame him. His parents had divorced not long before, and he was just beginning to figure out where he fit in his new junior high social scene. His parents had split custody, so he generally spent an even amount of time at each household, shuttling between his remarried father's house, with its new baby, and his mother's place. When I asked him to rank the most important things he was dealing with, he said, "IM, text messaging, the new dog at his mom's house, and skateboarding." When I quizzed him about how he handled homework, he admitted that he had pretty much just given up. He didn't have a particularly set schedule for when he would be at which house, and besides, it was constantly changing due to his mother's frequent business trips and his father's work schedule. To make matters worse, often after being dropped off at one home he'd discover that he'd left important textbooks, schoolwork, or his computer behind at the other.

His mother was the one who brought him to me for help. She was a designer and fairly organized, if a little scattered. She wanted Jeremy to be more on top of his own assignments and responsibilities and was unsure of how to help him develop a system that would work with his current two-home environment. Jeremy's father was far more lenient in terms of schoolwork and study and was initially quite resistant to the process. He believed that Jeremy was doing fine, that he was a typical boy, and that schoolwork was not that big of a deal. At his father's house, Jeremy did not even have a set place to study—the dining room table was filled with piles of paper, and there was no desk in his bedroom. The kitchen was always noisy and busy with the new baby, who at a moment's notice would erupt in a shriek, ending any slim opportunity for concentration.

One Monday afternoon early in our time working together, Jeremy had finally had enough. He had a big project due on Thursday but he didn't know at which house he'd be spending Wednesday night. This was a problem because not only was the project difficult to transport from one house to another but his mom's house had most of the supplies he needed and his dad's house didn't. When we asked him to map out his upcoming week's schedule, he broke down in tears, and who could blame him?

After about six months, both parents were able to be more forward planning about which nights Jeremy would spend at each house, so he didn't feel constantly in a state of flux. On Sunday night, he would look at his planner and spend fifteen to twenty minutes mapping out his week in terms of which night he would be where and what that meant in terms of his soccer cleats, gym shorts, and his trombone. Even though he had occasional slip-ups and was not always able to anticipate upcoming challenges, Jeremy overall felt more in control of his schedule, which gave him both the opportunity to begin thinking about achieving the goals he had set for himself, and more time to relax.

Even though each parent had a different style and living situations, Jeremy and I mapped out what he needed at each home in order to be organized and prepared to complete his homework and study for tests. At his mom's, he did his homework at the dining room table—a quiet spot but not completely sequestered, yet still free of distractions like his computer. As for Dad's, he and his father cleared out space in the downstairs family room—away from where the new baby spent most of her day—and put his desk and relevant study materials there. Because his books were heavy and it was cumbersome to carry them all around everywhere (especially because like most junior high students he did not have a locker), his parents agreed to purchase an extra set of used textbooks online so he had a set at each home.

> Even though each parent had a different style and living situation, Jeremy and I mapped out what he needed at each home in order to be organized and prepared to complete his homework and study for tests.

Jeremy's parents also agreed to some changes in routine and expectations so that he wouldn't have to struggle to shift between two different households with vastly different rules. Both households eventually adopted a routine in which Jeremy does his homework in a two-hour block (with a break every thirty minutes) and that he does not watch television or play video games on weekdays. After finishing his homework, Jeremy is able to spend some time on the computer or hanging out with his friends who live in the neighborhood. Both parents realized that as long as Jeremy knew what to expect and had some sort of regular structure within the different households, he was able to manage switching houses midweek without too many difficulties.

Tips for Two-Household Families

The following strategies should help your son stay on track and manage his responsibilities. I'm confident you'll find that these strategies will dovetail nicely with techniques you're already using to coordinate with your parenting partner.

Double Up on Essential Tools and Supplies

One of the most challenging issues for Jeremy was something that wasn't terribly complicated to fix. His father's home did not have the same supplies that he needed for school as his mom's house did—so if he needed glue sticks, construction paper, and markers for an assignment while at his dad's, he was out of luck. After his dad set up the desk in the family room and stocked it with the necessary supplies, there was one less burden for Jeremy.

Some parents ask me if buying a second set of textbooks is worth it—and my answer depends on the particular student's situation. For some students, especially those in the younger grades, it can be particularly helpful. If it's financially possible for you to do so, buying a second set of textbooks (used books can often be found cheaper on-line, and can be resold at the end of the school year) can reduce the hassle of schlepping textbooks from one home to another. Like Jeremy, many junior high students do not have lockers, so carrying around all their textbooks every day can be an overwhelming burden. The only problem I have found occurs when students are asked to write and take notes in their textbooks—having two sets of books can mean that the notes are split between two textbooks, which is unhelpful.

Create a Consistent Transition Plan

Adrian's parents divorced when he was seven years old, and his mom has since remarried. Now a freshman in high school, Adrian's parents have a split custody arrangement in which he spends Sunday to Monday at his mom's, Tuesday and Wednesday at his dad's, and Thursday at his mom's. His Friday and Saturday nights then alternate between parents. When I first heard about his schedule, I thought that Adrian would be overwhelmed by the constant shifting, but he wasn't. In fact, he picked up on our organizational strategies fairly quickly (especially for a freshman) and was motivated to reach his goals and do well in school.

One reason for his success was that he and his parents had developed a consistent transition plan from one house to another, with flexibility to accommodate Adrian's needs. Each day, he brought whatever he needed to school, used his locker, and was picked up by the parent whose house he was sleeping at that evening. Because his parents lived five minutes away from each other, he had a safety net in case anything was forgotten, but that was not often a problem. Al-

One reason for his success was that he and his parents had developed a consistent transition plan from one house to another, with flexibility to accommodate Adrian's needs.

though Adrian's arrangement would not be ideal for every student or parent, one of the reasons it worked so well for Adrian is that they had a consistent transition routine, which helped simplify everyone's life.

Develop a Schedule That Works Well for Both You and Your Son

Riley's parents also had joint custody, but quickly found that transitioning in the middle of the week or every other weekend did not work well for them or for Riley. Instead, he spends the entire week and the following weekend at one parent's house, transitioning from one house to the other on Monday afternoons after school. Riley and his parents find this helps with scheduling, particularly in terms of seeing friends, making weekend plans, and working on long-term projects. Riley is a young man who really needs a consistent routine, and his parents worked together to find a solution that works well for them and for him.

Compare Notes

The vast majority of families I talked with agreed that getting together with their son's other household to compare notes is essential for maintaining a structure that works for everyone, especially their son.

Suzanne is a grandmother who plays a significant role in the raising of her grandson Tommy. In fact, I have never had a conversation with Tommy's mother, Lisa; Suzanne is the one who signed Tommy up to work with me, drives him to my office, and keeps in contact with me about everything.

Tommy is in the seventh grade at a local parochial school and is a warm and excited young man who typically bounces into my office with a beaming smile and a good story. Tommy stays with Suzanne a few nights a week while Lisa travels for work, so he lives in two different households.

In the beginning, it was tough for Tommy to adjust going back to his mom's house, because Suzanne's home is much more structured and, being retired, she's always available to help him with anything and everything. At Suzanne's house, Tommy is the main focus. Conversely, Lisa has a demanding job and travels two weeks out of the month, and with the lack of structure and understandable chaos this brings, Tommy initially had trouble getting work done at his mother's house. Typically, Tommy would leave his grandmother's house fully supported and prepared, only to return a week later having to, in his grandmother's opinion, "start all over again."

Over time, Suzanne and Lisa learned to share information: what Tommy was working on, how Tommy worked best, and what he had upcoming. Suzanne jotted notes on a piece of yellow legal pad paper, and give Lisa bullet points regarding school, sports, and other upcoming events so Tommy could successfully transition from one household to the other. They readjusted their routines so there was similar structure at both homes in terms of doing homework, free time, relaxing, and being organized. Comparing notes alleviated Lisa's stress when she came home from a business trip because she immediately knew what was going on and what she needed to address, and Suzanne was able to feel like she didn't have to start all over again every time Tommy came back to stay with her for a few days.

> Over time, Suzanne and Lisa learned to share information: what Tommy was working on, how Tommy worked best, and what he had upcoming.

Communicate with Your Parenting Partner

Especially if your son is in junior high or in his first years of high school, he may be trying to juggle long-term projects or group assignments with the fact that he is at his dad's for the weekend. If he spends every other weekend at his dad's, he may want to forgo his schoolwork so as not to miss that crucial time. Communicate the steps you are taking to help your son become more organized, and strategize with the other parent as to what he or she can do to foster a more consistent routine. When things come up or if you foresee conflicts (a huge group project due on Monday and the entire group lives closer to one parent than the other), anticipate what you can do to make changes.

Having a joint online calendar (such as a Gmail calendar) or a similar wall calendar that hangs at both homes can be especially helpful for students and parents to juggle the additional organizational challenges created by a multi-household arrangement. This calendar then holds the child's schedule and can be accessed and edited by all concerned, so that everyone can be up to date on upcoming soccer games, sleepovers, and other major events. It can even be used to block out and schedule time for homework, especially when students are shifting between two homes. If you are not comfortable using the computer, a wall calendar is a perfectly fine alternative—just make sure that when you update something on your calendar, it gets updated on the calendar in the other home.

Be Flexible

Although establishing a unified structure and routine is important, it's also essential to maintain some flexibility in order to respond to situations that arise. Often when one parent can't fulfill a specific obligation, there's a tendency for the other to dig in his or her heels and point to the agreed-upon routine. Too often the child ends up missing out on an opportunity in those cases. That's unfortunate, and preventable. Keep the bigger picture—your son's well-being and enrichment—front and center, and work together to make sure his needs are met.

Summary

Household transitions are stressful to any student, but especially so for one who struggles with organization. Whether the change is due to divorce, separation, or a big change to an existing household structure, parents often underestimate the impact these kinds of changes can have on a young person whose plate is already very full.

Things to keep in mind:

- Find ways to make simple things easier; it's hard enough for a child to keep to an academic schedule without having to wonder if he'll have the right books or materials on hand, or have a place to work. Make sure the basics are covered.

- Create a consistent transition plan. Most kids don't want to worry about how they'll get from point A to point B. Let them concentrate on other issues.

- Develop a schedule that works well for both you and your son while staying somewhat flexible; the less stress on all players, the better.

- Compare notes and communicate with your parenting partner. You're both part of your child's successes and disappointments, and a good open line of communication can assuage a lot of potential problems.

12

Special Considerations

Illness

Because I've worked for many years with junior high and high school students, I like to think that I have a Teflon-like immune system. I eat well, exercise, do lots of yoga, and try to minimize stress, and I generally tend to avoid most of the nasty bugs when they come around the office. A few years ago, after flying down to L.A. for a few days, I contracted an ugly flu, one of those nasty ones that can leave you completely incoherent for at least a week. Within twenty-four hours, I was down for the count, unable to move off my couch for four days. Even my stubborn terrier, Mason, who typically insists on thrice-daily walks to our neighborhood park, looked at me with pity when I could barely walk to the front door and let him out. I was a complete disaster.

Here's the important thing; as soon as I became sick, I completely cleared my schedule, determined not to get back to work before I was able to function normally. "Nobody wants whatever flu I have," I told everyone. "You'll thank me for sparing you." Most people were grateful and actually *did* thank me, especially after hearing my depressing voice on the phone. My associates picked up the appointments that they could, and I canceled the rest. I had never before missed that many days at the office, but as an adult who teaches time-management and organization for a living, it was pretty easy for me to devise a plan to get back on track as soon as I felt better. The following week I returned to the office, rested and recuperated. Within a week of being back, I managed to catch up with most everything that I had missed, and life was back to normal.

Most kids who get sick are not that lucky. Because missing even a few days from school can lead to missed assignments and increased stress, I often see intelligent and well-meaning parents, fearful that their child will fall behind, send their sick kids to school. These children, whose grim disposition and pale countenance gives new meaning to the term *ghostly*, are unable to do much in the classroom beyond spreading their germs. In the end, they fall behind anyway, take longer to get better, and generally make everyone around them miserable.

Short-Term Illness: Cold, Flu, Strep, and Other Ailments

They are so overwhelmed by the prospect of having to make up work while keeping up with new assignments, many would gladly throw in the towel and start over next semester when they have a fresh start.

A 2007 Centers for Disease Control and Prevention (CDC) survey found that the vast majority of children miss five days or less of school per year, most of which is due to short-term illness. For some kids, just missing school is stressful and overwhelming, in addition to whatever discomfort they suffered while sick. Often when these students recover and come into my office, the first thing I have to do is calm them down. They are so overwhelmed by the prospect of having to make up work while keeping up with new assignments, many would gladly throw in the towel and start over next semester when they have a fresh start. I help them get back on track not by doubling their workload but by simply adjusting their organizational strategies—the same ones they've been using all year long.

If your son misses school due to illness, following these general guidelines will not only get him up to speed sooner but will do it while decreasing stress, both for him *and* for you.

Let Sick Kids Rest

You may remember that when I first introduced Tim, the Over-Scheduled Procrastinator, I mentioned that he tended to get sick a lot. The truth is that every winter, without fail, he would catch a cold, which would invariably morph into a flu-like virus that hung around for weeks. One of the reasons he never really got better is that he never truly took a break. Some days he would go to school late and miss a few classes, but then play in a basketball match after school. Other days, he would miss tennis practice but still go to school. If he missed the entire day of school, he was at home working on details for the prom or trying to finish up a big project that he had left for the last minute. He'd spend most of his winters half sick, missing a day here and a day there, but never feeling 100 percent healthy and *always* stressed out about the effect this was having on his life.

One reason Tim spent so much time on this roller coaster is that he never gave himself the chance to completely recuperate, leaving his immune system compromised and open to catching something far worse. In fact, in the middle of his junior year—a particularly stressful year—he went through the same cycle but this time he ended up contracting a scary case of pneumonia, from which it took him weeks to fully recover. The good news was that by his senior year—and perhaps this was in part because he was a senior, and the stress of college applications was behind him—Tim finally started to really give himself a rest. When he was sick with a cold, he took three days off from school and didn't go back to his after-school activities until he felt completely better. Not only did he end up feeling healthier for most of his spring semester but he also ended up missing less school overall because he took three full days off when he was sick instead of spreading it out over three weeks of up-and-down health.

> If your child has a bad cold or flu, keep him home and let him sleep, sip soup, and watch mindless television as appropriate.

If your child has a bad cold or flu, keep him home and let him sleep, sip soup, and watch mindless television as appropriate. Don't send him to soccer practice, youth group, or the school dance. While he's home sick, let him focus his efforts on getting better rather than trying to comprehend the new math concept or finishing the English essay. In the end, he will get better more quickly and be less likely to get sick again.

Another thing to remember is that if you send your sick child to school, chances are that he will be operating at less than full capacity and may miss nearly as much information as he would have if he'd stayed home. Trouble is, because he was there physically, he probably won't be eligible for the same kind of makeup support that he would have if he'd stayed home; a lose–lose situation.

Empower Him to Be Proactive with Teachers to Establish Deadlines

Whenever Scott got sick, his mom would immediately contact all of his teachers and ask for his missing assignments, leaving copies of their email responses on his desk for him. She had no trouble figuring out the ways in which he could make up his assignments and get back on track; she was an incredibly organized person and managing was what she did best. In fact, the teachers were so impressed they never bothered to ask Scott to come see them about what he'd missed; after all, Mom was on top of it.

Unfortunately, her approach was dead on arrival. Scott, annoyed with his mom's interference and stressed by the fact that he had to make up so much work, threw all the correspondence, unread, into the trash. Because he did not have ownership of his own process he was unable to concentrate on what he had to do and focused instead on his mother's meddling. Over time, though, Scott's mom came to realize that having him take care of his own schoolwork would be more efficient and that, despite a few hiccups, he would be better able to manage the process if he had complete ownership of it. Scott was able to become more proactive about taking control of his makeup assignments and schedule and was able to negotiate with teachers to juggle all the different assignments and makeup tests and quizzes appropriately.

> Over time, though, Scott's mom came to realize that having him take care of his own schoolwork would be more efficient and that, despite a few hiccups, he would be better able to manage the process if he had complete ownership of it.

Once your child feels better, encourage him to talk to teachers and figure out when missed assignments are due and how tests and quizzes can be made up; emailing teachers right away is a good idea; it shows responsibility and fosters good will. Your son's school guidance counselor can also be of great assistance, but again, your son needs to be proactive in seeking out the guidance counselor's help. I know that it may seem easier for you to send off a quick email to take care of it, but allowing your son to manage as much of the process as he can by himself will enable him to build resiliency and independence. Sometimes, parents worry that the teachers are not fair or adequately understanding of their individual's child's situation and that as parents they can get a better outcome than if the student sought out the teacher directly. In some rare cases this may be true, but mostly I find that teachers are understanding and compassionate if a student is proactive and readily communicates his needs. Generally, getting one day for every day missed is fair; so if your child missed four school days, he should get four school days to make up the work (preferably with a weekend in between).

Have Him Devise a Master To-Do List

After he gets better, have him devise a master to-do list. In my office, one of the first things I have students do when they come in after missing school is to have them create a master to-do list. On a blank piece of paper, I have them list every single class and compile every assignment that needs to get caught up in the class. Some schools have homework online, while others require students to gather assignments directly from teachers. Having it all written down in one place may initially make them feel slightly more overwhelmed, but just listing everything and doing a brain dump will help them begin the process of getting caught up. Depending on your relationship with your child, you may or may not be the best person to help devise this master list. Perhaps he can devise this list on his own, but I have found that even older children like someone to sit by them while they empty their brain of all the assignments, tests, quizzes, and long-term projects. If someone else would be better to help them with this process (older sibling, tutor), by all means outsource.

Have Him Split Up the Assignments

After Tim listed all of the assignments that he had to make up, we looked to see what he could complete relatively easily, and he went after those assignments first. He split all of the work over four days, leaving the easiest, smallest assignments first, and the larger, more cumbersome assignments for the weekend. For instance, Tim found math to be relatively straightforward, so he completed his three overdue math assignments right away, getting one class completely finished so he could focus on whatever else needed to be done. It gave him a sense of accomplishment to cross the easy assignments off his list and also gave him momentum to work on the more challenging assignments. He knew that once he was done with the physics project, he'd have made up everything and would be back on track. By the following Monday, he was completely caught up, and the entire process was less stressful than he had originally imagined.

Next to each assignment on your son's master to-do list, have him note the day on which he'll tackle that particular task. I have always found that being less aggressive (for example, scheduling fewer assignments each day so that your son may be encouraged to get started) is much better than scheduling too many makeup assignments and consequently having him feel intimidated. Scheduling when the makeup work will be done will help him feel less anxious and overwhelmed, and he can focus on simply tackling one assignment at a time.

> Scheduling when the makeup work will be done will help him feel less anxious and overwhelmed, and he can focus on simply tackling one assignment at a time.

Set Aside Additional Blocks of Time for Makeup Homework

Set aside an additional block of time each night and a few extra blocks over the weekend just for working on makeup assignments. One of the things Scott found most helpful in getting himself caught up was having a designated period of time to focus just on makeup work. After he missed two days of school with a bad cold, he wrote down each of the makeup assignments he had to complete. For the next two nights, he spent two hours on his homework and then took an hour-long break. Even though coming back to do a second two-hour block of work was not ideal, he was able to get completely caught up in all of his classes by the end of the week.

Instead of lumping in the makeup work with all the current assignments, encourage your child to set aside specific time every day to work on it. Each time, he should focus on only a few makeup assignments from the master to-do list. Just like scheduling baseball practice or flute lessons, scheduling two or three two-hour blocks over the weekend after your child feels better can help him get a lot of work done without worrying about it. Just make sure he also plans on having some fun or relaxing time outside the extra homework time.

Have Him Use His Planner to Track Missed Assignments

After Tim had created his master to-do list and figured out what day he was going to get each assignment done, he went through and wrote down each makeup assignment on the corresponding day in his planner. In doing so, he further simplified and streamlined his process of making up work, because he was able to look at each day and focus only on the assignments that he was planning on working on that day (in addition to his regular schoolwork). For him, it was an important way of taking the overwhelming bigger picture—too many assignments to make up and not enough time to do it—and compartmentalizing it into smaller, more manageable chunks.

Your son should choose makeup assignments from his master list and put them in his planner on the day he is planning on doing them. Encourage him to put numbers by each assignment so that he can roughly plan out the order in which he will complete them. He should then draw a small box next to each assignment so that he can check it off when he is done.

Clear the Calendar of After-School Extras for the First Few Days Your Son Is Back at School

One of the reasons that Tim battled being sick for so long was that he dove back into things too early. He was usually at school at 7:00 a.m. for a student council meeting and had tennis practice until about 6:00 p.m. Before he had even started his homework, he had already completed an eleven-hour day. With homework and makeup work, it easily stretched into a fourteen-hour day, and that was just days after he had been unable to even get out of bed. As a result of those punishingly long hours, he wreaked havoc on his already weakened immune system.

Just because your son feels well enough to go back to school doesn't mean that he is necessarily ready to juggle all the different activities that may be on his plate. He may want to dive back into sports and extra-curricular activities, but clearing the calendar can give his body extra time to recuperate. His immunity is probably still low and taking a few more days before returning to a full plate will help him avoid getting sick again. You may also find that he needs that time to implement the extra makeup time mentioned previously.

Some students complain to me that their coach won't let them miss practice or that their coach insists that if they are well enough to go to school, then they are well enough to attend practice. In the long run, missing a few practices to get back to optimal shape more quickly should be the coach's goal, because illnesses and injuries can often become more problematic and intense if not addressed properly in the beginning.

> In the long run, missing a few practices to get back to optimal shape more quickly should be the coach's goal, because illnesses and injuries can often become more problematic and intense if not addressed properly in the beginning.

Chronic, Long-Term, and Life-Threatening Illnesses

For many years, I have spent one or two weeks each summer volunteering as a camp counselor with children who have chronic and life-threatening illnesses. Being at camp is always one of the most exhilarating, inspiring, and exhausting weeks of my year, and it never fails to rejuvenate me. More important, over the course of the week, the combination of fresh air, new adventures, and endless social opportunities transforms the campers in ways that many would have had trouble even imagining—in a word, it's magical.

Research has found that anywhere from 18 to 20 percent of all children suffer from a chronic illness, and of those more than half will be forced to regularly miss school. Some will miss only a day here and there; kids with type 1 diabetes, which is becoming more common in otherwise healthy children, average an additional three sick days a year over their healthy counterparts, which may be just often enough to throw them off track. Kids with asthma miss a bit more—on average, nearly four days a year. Other kids with more debilitating illnesses may leave school for months at a time to receive treatment or because their bodies can't handle the rigors of a full school day. Besides the gaps in schoolwork, having a long-term or chronic illness can be debilitating to a student's sense that he can get organized and manage his time because even with the best of intentions, something can always go awry and a treatment can be changed, postponed, or oth-

> Besides the gaps in schoolwork, having a long-term or chronic illness can be debilitating to a student's sense that he can get organized and manage his time because even with the best of intentions, something can always go awry and a treatment can be changed, postponed, or otherwise thwarted.

erwise thwarted. In addition, he may feel intellectually and socially alienated, either because his absences cause him to miss out on the social aspects of school, or simply that he feels different because of his illness.

As parents, one of the best things that you can do is help create a support system of advocates and advisers within your child's educational and medical settings to ensure that he has some element of control, choice, and routine within the ever-changing, stressful, and often overwhelming situation of being sick with a chronic or long-term illness. Keep in mind, also, the following strategies.

Be Flexible

When a child is struggling with the exhausting effects of a chronic or long-term illness, it may not be possible for him to focus on school-work as intently as when he was healthy. Kids may appear to be okay to their teachers and classmates and yet be physically, emotionally, and mentally exhausted, and the course load and class choices that worked last year may now be overwhelming. It's important for parents and school counselors to recognize that anything that can make a child's life easier and more manageable should be explored, including adjustments to course schedules. Especially at the beginning of an illness, parents often need to help their child understand that they deserve accommodations and that it is not a sign of weakness to make adjustments or to take less strenuous classes. Some students have a hard time with this because if they were once in all honors classes, it's difficult to realize that those classes might be too much work right now, and they become frustrated with feeling less intelligent or less capable than they were when they were healthy.

One of the important messages for parents and school counselors to convey is that these temporary accommodations—and I like to use the word *temporary*, even if "temporary" stretches out to years—do not mean that the student is any less smart, rather that making the right accommodations at the right time helps ensure that the young person is set up to succeed. In the midst of dealing with the wide range of emotional and social issues that often accompany dealing with chronic illnesses, feeling in control of their school options is an important way for these kids to create power within a powerless situation.

Years ago, I worked with an eighth grader named Greg who was dealing with a recent diagnosis of Crohn's disease. Greg was shorter and smaller than most of the kids his age, and physically looked about three years younger than his eighth grade peers. Well-liked and social, and loved among the girls in his class, he felt insecure about his small stature. When I first met him, I could tell that he was highly intelligent and motivated to do well in school, but it was also clear that he was incredibly disorganized. During our time working together, he was shuttling through doctors and specialists to try to figure out what exactly he had that was causing him so much pain (when we first met, he had yet to be diagnosed).

For Greg, his ability to get work done depended on the type of week he was having physically; when he felt okay, he was able to get a satisfactory amount of work done; nothing stellar, but everything was turned in on time and there were no desperate errors or oversights. On weeks when his body was really ravaged, almost nothing would get done; he didn't finish homework assignments, he'd flunk tests and quizzes, and he'd generally act as if he were a bump on a log. But because he was attending school and "looked" okay, the teachers initially thought he was being lazy and unmotivated.

Even after his diagnosis, as doctors changed his medications and treatment regimens, and Greg was on a roller coaster of physical and mental emotions, concentrating on algebra was the least of his concerns. Midway through his eighth grade year, doctors put him on prednisone, which caused his face to swell unrecognizably and his weight to balloon by over sixty pounds—not exactly the ideal situation for an eighth grade boy on the verge of puberty and concerned about his physical appearance. By the end of most school days, Greg was so drained that the idea of studying for an upcoming history test or proactively making flash cards was a fantasy somewhere between making the All-Star baseball team and asking out the girl who sat next to him in his English class.

Finally, the school guidance counselor talked with Greg and his parents about the many ways in which his energy and time were being currently expended on doctor's visits, new medications, and juggling all that additional stress and how that detracted from being able to take on time-consuming classes and electives. Working with the guidance counselor, Greg and his parents were able to come up with a plan in which his schedule would be temporarily modified. Even though these modifications would leave him ineligible for Spanish 2 and honors geometry as a high school freshman, everyone looked at the big picture and realized how his physical and emotional abilities had changed over the past three months. His teachers gave him extended time on tests (something that he would not have needed when he was healthy). Some days, when he was particularly tired, he went go into the nurse's office to rest on the couch for thirty minutes to an hour before heading back to class.

> Working with the guidance counselor, Greg and his parents were able to come up with a plan in which his schedule would be temporarily modified.

At home, we lightened his homework load so that he would do three thirty-minute blocks of homework between 5:00 and 7:00 p.m. He would sometimes take a nap before he started his work, and most nights he would be in bed before 10:00. He still followed most of the structure of the homework and organizational system, but he modified it according to how his body felt. Knowing that he had a system he could rely on, which was modifiable and flexible, made him feel more empowered and in control of his situation, so that when he was feeling good again, he could easily figure out how to get back on track. Was the situation perfect? No, but it made Greg feel more powerful in an uncontrollable situation, which was incredibly important. It made him feel he could do his best at that particular time, rather than feeling so overwhelmed that it would be easier to just give up.

In addition to using the resource room and taking extended time on tests, some students find that taking a break of some sort during the day or having a shortened day (where they go home before or after lunch) can help them get through school easier when their energy is depleted and their mind is drained. Though some students would prefer to be home-schooled, others want to be able to go to school. Depending on your child's individual circumstances, finding accommodations can make the school part of being sick more manageable and less overwhelming.

Empower Your Child to Educate Teachers and Classmates

When I was in the first grade, my classmate Beth, whom I had known since I was a toddler, had to have a radical brain surgery operation called a hemispherectomy to remove half of her brain. She had been struggling with numerous seizures (which we all knew about), and the surgery was the one thing that would help her lead a long life. Before the surgery, I remember that the school nurse came in and talked to us in great depth about what was going to happen and answered all of our questions. In doing so, it made us less fearful and more understanding of Beth and why she was out of school so often. We weren't told all the scary things that could have happened, but we felt we knew what was going on, instead of having to rely on whispers and half-truths from adults. I remember spending one morning class creating get-well-soon cards and pictures for her, and then spending my own money to buy her a card and send her a coloring book because I figured she must be bored sleeping all the time at the hospital. By educating us about her process, we gained a heightened sensitivity and understanding for her needs, which normalized the experience for us as best as could be. (*Update:* Today Beth works as a kindergarten assistant at our old elementary school.)

Giving your child with a chronic or life-altering illness the option to be a part of the education process can be empowering because he can feel he is teaching his classmates about his experience. Sallie Sanborn, a New York City therapist who works with children and families who are dealing with chronic, life-threatening and life-limiting illnesses often goes into schools and classrooms to give educational presentations when a child is sick. Whenever Sanborn gives a presentation to a classroom, she always offers the child the opportunity to stand up with her. A few times, after starting out sitting in the back, the child starts to answers his classmates' questions and takes over the presentation as he becomes more comfortable speaking about his issues. Unfortunately, schools don't always have a lot of experience dealing with the psycho-social issues surrounding chronic and life-threatening illnesses. If it is appropriate, having your son be part of the educating process for his class and school can be tremendously empowering for him and can normalize the experience for his classmates, helping make them more aware and sensitive to the issues he's facing.

> If it is appropriate, having your son be part of the educating process for his class and school can be tremendously empowering for him, and can normalize the experience to his classmates, helping to make them more aware and sensitive to the issues he's facing.

Create a Flexible Routine

Keeping the needs of your child in mind, create a routine around what he is able to do and how he is best able to get things done. One of my students with type 1 diabetes was struggling in his chemistry class, in part because it was early in the morning and mornings can be sluggish for diabetics as their bodies attempt to adjust their blood glucose levels from their daily insulin injection. We talked about it, and he decided that he would try to switch into a chemistry class that met later in the morning and have his studio art class for his first period. He enjoyed art, and it didn't require the note taking and mathematical analysis that he needed for chemistry. It was an easy switch (well, admittedly, schedule changes are never easy) that enabled him to be in the class when he was most able to concentrate.

Using the organizational and time-management techniques highlighted in earlier chapters, you can create a flexible routine that can be adjusted as appropriate for your child's challenges and struggles. For instance, if you know that school wears him out and he is tired when he comes home, have him take a nap for a few hours and rest before doing any schoolwork. If you know that he concentrates best during the late morning, have him schedule an hour of homework each weekend day during that time so that he can rest when he is exhausted.

Monitor Each Situation As It Unfolds

If it seems your son is not getting work done because he is tired or unmotivated, look at the whole picture. When there are complex health issues, every bit of behavior is information and should be part of an assessment. Sometimes kids act as though they are giving up when in reality they may just be undergoing an especially reflective and thoughtful period, one they may not necessarily want to tell their parents about. Parents, on the other hand, sometimes struggle to keep things the same because they're afraid that any small change is the start of a larger, more significant decline.

Sanborn told me the story of a sixteen-year-old high school junior with a brain tumor. Though he had an invasive brain surgery a year earlier, he was doing well and looked physically healthy. Every month, he missed a few days of school to visit his doctor in New York City, get a scan, and have a thorough checkup. One day he announced to his parents that he no longer wanted to go to school. At first, they were frustrated because it seemed on the surface that he was giving up, but after talking to him for a while, the truth emerged. He told them that he was frustrated that he had to spend six hours every day, often when he wasn't feeling well, sitting upright in a chair at school. There were days when his body's reaction to his medication made it unbearable to be at school, and other days when he was so exhausted by midmorning that he just trudged along, lifeless and dejected, through the rest of the day.

With Sanborn's help, the young man, his parents, and the school designed a plan that involved home-schooling with a tutor a few days a week and finding ways to pursue his outside interests during the day when he felt healthiest. This was a very positive step: He was regaining some power and control over the illness that had taken over much of his life, and the combination of home-schooling and outside interests enabled him to become reengaged and invested in his educational opportunities both inside and outside the classroom.

Seek Support to Make Sure Your Child's Needs Are Addressed

When necessary, seek outside support to make sure that your child's needs are advocated for and addressed. Depending on your child's school situation, a school counselor or other advocate can help address needs that you may not even be aware of and can make certain transitions easier. Often, having a counselor or therapist recognize the immediate needs of the child is more effective than having parents, who are often dealing with their own range of emotions and challenges, advocate within the school setting. Children may be open about their needs, concerns, and fears with a counselor or a therapist because they are less worried about their parent's feelings and more able to focus on figuring out their own needs and wants. As Sanborn says, "Our kids protect us from their difficult feelings, and they shouldn't have to." She often works with families and schools to figure out what students need and are entitled to at various stages of their illness, and she often sees parents who don't realize or recognize what services their child is entitled to and what accommodations would make being in school easier for their son.

> As Sanborn says, "Our kids protect us from their difficult feelings, and they shouldn't have to."

Listen to What Your Son Really Wants

This may seem simplistic and obvious, but it's amazing to me the number of times I talk to parents of sick children who have never really asked their child what he wants or what would make his life easier in terms of schooling. Children who are sick are entitled to and need to express a broad range of emotions because being happy and positive all the time takes a lot of energy. Developmentally, some younger kids might want to go to school despite their illness because they feel that it's a fun place to be. Socially, some teens may want to go to school even though they feel pretty crappy and are not able to get all the schoolwork done because they don't want to miss out on the social element of school. Still others may want to leave formal schooling and be home-schooled for a period of time so that they can explore their own outside interests.

If your child is struggling with a chronic or life-threatening condition, allowing him to reveal his desires and priorities enables him to gain some control over his situation. Even if all of his wishes can't come true (after all, we can't all leave school and join the traveling circus) some accommodations and adjustments can often be made to address and recognize what he is hoping for, within the school setting and beyond.

Take a Break from Schooling

Sometimes, it's just not possible for a student to keep coming to school; his treatment is leaving him exhausted, and his health is unpredictable and challenging. In those cases, you and your child, along with school officials, might decide that having a teacher come to the home a few hours a week is a better option. Your child's course load could also be modified to accommodate his needs, and he could create a routine to keep him organized and able to finish whatever needs to get accomplished. For instance, on days that he is feeling well, have him do four half-hour increments of work during the time of day when he generally feels best, and then let him do whatever he wants for the rest of the time.

When a child leaves school for a number of months, the social experience is suddenly missing. Instead of walking through the hallways seeing his peers, he is sitting at home spending hours on the couch. If your son enjoys the social aspect of school, being at home can be especially isolating. Find a way for him to be socially engaged—whether through an activity, or perhaps via rotating visits from friends—and make sure he helps devise it so that it's in line with what he wants. For many boys, social networking sites might help them feel a little more connected because even if they can't see their school friends every day, they can see what's happening online.

When a child gets ready to go back to school after a number of months, it's important that you address the details of reentry in a way in which he feels comfortable. One child Sanborn worked with attended

When a child gets ready to go back to school after a number of months, it's important that you address the details of reentry in a way in which he feels comfortable.

a middle school that had its morning announcements shown on video, and when he returned to school after a few months of treatment for leukemia, he was part of that morning show. Another middle school student had the child life specialist from the hospital come with him on his first day back to talk with the class.

At the high school level, reentry options may depend on the size and setup of your son's school. After being away for several months, your son might have unrealistic expectations of what school will be like, and his classmates might have exaggerated fears of what has happened to their classmate. Some things probably changed while he was away, and it can be disconcerting to just plop back into class after being away for several months. Working with a school counselor or administrator can be helpful in determining the best course.

Also, it's good to remember that students who may have been on an honors track or otherwise accelerated courses may not be able to return to those advanced classes if they've been away for a time. While it may be tough for the student to acknowledge that track may no longer be available to him, it's good to accept that the *pace* of learning isn't that important. In other words, it's not crucial that your son takes calculus in high school rather than in college (where most kids learn it); it's just important that he takes it at some point in his educational career (depending on his future plans).

When a Parent/Family Member Is Sick or Dies

Late into his junior year of high school, Damian's father was struggling with pancreatic cancer and passed away within a year of his initial diagnosis. Damian was incredibly close to his father, a successful real estate developer who before falling ill had attended every one of his son's football and basketball games. Needless to say, Damian's Sincere Slacker habits devolved to a complete and utter loss of ability to think, process, and function. When his father was sick, he went to school most days with his eyes glazed over, and his teachers—not knowing the full extent of his family's struggles and loss—attributed his behavior to an exaggeration of his previous low-energy manner.

His parents hadn't talked about the very real possibility that Damian's father was going to die until a few months after his diagnosis, but in the interim Damian had done an Internet search and was well informed, even though he didn't share his feelings with his parents or other family members. Early on, even his parents were confused as to why he had three Ds and an F on his midterm report card. "Didn't Damian know how important junior year grades were?" they asked me with a trace of anger in their voices. In the midst of all this stress, Damian's back went out and he could no longer play basketball; in fact, this once active teenager wasn't able to do anything involving running and jumping for eight weeks.

When I saw Damian, there was little confusion as to why he was struggling so much in school. His mind was both racing and empty all at once, and nothing seemed to matter to him anymore. The last thing Damian wanted to concentrate on during his father's rapidly deteriorating condition was turning in homework assignments and reading irrelevant (to him) schoolbooks. Most days, Damian would come home and sit at the dining room table, and stare at a page for ten minutes. Getting anything done seemed impossible and overwhelming.

> The last thing Damian wanted to concentrate on during his father's rapidly deteriorating condition was turning in homework assignments and reading irrelevant (to him) schoolbooks.

Damian and I talked about what a struggle it was to focus on school, and just validating his concerns and feelings toward school and homework made him feel calmer. I helped him look at the big picture (that things were tough now and that was okay), and with his parent's support, he started to work with a grief counselor. We also realized that even with his back injury he could still swim and work out on a stationary bike, and soon there he was, at the Y four or five days a week, swimming and cycling. We figured out the list of work that his teachers would allow him to make up, and he started to go to the library several times a week for two hours at a time because his house no longer felt like an easy place to concentrate. Damian finished out the year without any Ds or Fs, which, given all he was dealing with in his family and with his own health, I considered a tremendous success. He was able to come up with temporary, flexible strategies that helped him do the best he could during a very difficult time.

> One of the questions I often ask kids in the office is, "Are you doing the best you can with what you've got?"

One of the questions I often ask kids in the office is, "Are you doing the best you can with what you've got?" It's actually a very freeing question. I am not asking them to be the best; rather I am asking them to try to be the best that they can be at that specific time.

Look for Outside Support

Sanborn strongly suggests that families with a sick or dying parent seek outside support very early ("on the day of diagnosis" she suggests). When a parent becomes sick or dies, the teen is not only struggling with the issues involving the loss of that parent but also with the loss of other family members as well, whose abilities and roles have changed because they are being a caretaker and/or are grieving themselves. Having a person who can advocate on your child's behalf, whether that is a social worker, school counselor, family friend or therapist, can enable your child to feel more supported as he adjusts to the changes that are occurring in his home and life. As Sanborn says, it's important to identify this outside support as early as possible, so that a foundation of trust and a helpful routine can be established before any further dramatic changes occur. Don't wait until the situation is a crisis to get help.

Maintain Consistency but Be Flexible

Keeping up a routine in terms of activities, homework time, and general household routines is really helpful for most kids, a little bit of normalcy amid the chaos. Keep the routine with the expectation that kids may not perform as well academically, athletically, or otherwise. Having distractions and regular outlets for stress—whether that be on the soccer team, in the band, or at a debate tournament—can help kids cope and find a sense of support.

Keep the School Up to Date on Changes

Often, children who are struggling with their parent's illness require temporary accommodations or academic modifications, working with a school counselor or a teacher in the same way you might if the student himself were ill. As much as possible, these accommodations should be flexible and open ended. Typically, a child will not want such accommodations because he doesn't want to stand out or appear different, but with his diminished ability to concentrate, extra time on tests and more one-on-one work can be essential for helping him get through the difficult time. An ad-

> Typically, a child will not want such accommodations because he doesn't want to stand out or appear different, but with his diminished ability to concentrate, extra time on tests and more one-on-one work can be essential for helping him get through the difficult time.

vocate should work with the school to stay aware of changes in the student's needs and to help him figure out what would serve him best.

Oftentimes, there is an immediate reaction for the first month after a parent's diagnosis or death, during which teachers are most forgiving of assignments and flexible with accommodations. But many of the students whom I work with have had really tough times six months, a year, or even three years after everyone gave them accommodations. As Sanborn notes, every trauma redefines itself throughout different stages of a person's life, and that is ever so true for children. As a child gains more cognitive awareness, the triggers for loss are not always as clean-cut as we would like them to be or think they should be. Those temporary accommodations might actually be most necessary a few months or years after the diagnosis or death of a parent.

Ask Your Child How He Wants to Tell the Class

When the parent of an elementary and middle school student is diagnosed with an illness, Sanborn often goes into the classroom and makes a presentation for all the students. She starts out her talk by asking how many kids know someone who has had a similar illness, such as cancer, and most times more than a few students raise their hands. That alone is a comforting fact for the child of an ill parent, and it also normalizes the experience so that he doesn't have to explain his situation. Kids often want to be comforting but don't always know what to say or do, so having someone come talk to the class can work well.

But remember, it really depends on the desires of the child. Some kids would prefer that books or materials be shared with the class, and others would rather not have anything happen at all, at least right away. In Sanborn's experience, feelings and decisions about how much to share with schoolmates can change over time.

Ask If the School Has a Template or Protocol

In an ideal world, all schools would have a protocol for how they handle a parent's illness or death within the school setting, and it would be individualized for the needs of each child and family. This template would include such topics as how to talk to a grieving child, how to create flexible expectations and temporary accommodations, and how to designate a point person within the school who the student can go to when he is having a breakdown and needs extra support—for some students it could be the school counselor, whereas other students may feel more comfortable with a teacher. Although every family illness or serious accident is unique, there are common issues and standard kinds of support any school can offer, and having it all organized in advance simply makes the process easier to implement.

> Although every family illness or serious accident is unique, there are common issues and standard kinds of support any school can offer, and having it all organized in advance simply makes the process easier to implement.

Summary

Dealing with an illness, whether short-term or chronic, can be challenging for any child. For the inevitable non-serious illnesses that strike all of us, remember to have your child rest and then be sensible and organized about getting him caught up with his schoolwork. It's not worth it to rush back or stress out; chances are he'll either be right back in bed or struggling to manage the work with depleted resources.

When your son's health is significantly compromised, remember that change will be inevitable, and it's best to meet it with flexibility. Advanced classes may have to give way to a more relaxed schedule, at least for a time. Get outside help and make sure you take your child's social needs into consideration. Also keep in mind that he may be the best advocate for his own situation when it comes to connecting with his peers.

If a family member or close friend of your child's is ill or passes away, don't be afraid to look for outside support. As with chronic illness, communication with your child is key.

13

Implementing the Strategies

Now that you have gone through all the tips and strategies, *you* might be feeling a little overwhelmed! You know your home and family dynamics best, so you're probably thinking about which strategies could easily be implemented in your situation (like creating a study space) and others that might take some time and effort (getting your son to eat breakfast, perhaps). As with anything else, *making sweeping long-term changes takes time*, especially when we are talking about a preteen or teenage boy. There will inevitably be starts and stops, so be patient and allow change to evolve gradually, and provide a built-in opportunity for boys to stop, regroup, refresh, and refocus.

As with the study skills presented in Chapter 8, the best way to introduce all this information to your son is *not all at once*! I hope that as you read the previous chapters, you began to think about how you and your son are going to work to incorporate the strategies in your home. In this chapter, you will find a sample five-week schedule of how you can introduce the strategies to your son. It may take longer for your student, and that's okay; the more gradual and consistent you are about making the changes, the more likely they will become a part of your lives rather than act as a quick-fix.

Remember the Importance of Attitude

When I work with boys, I don't get exasperated or frustrated if they come in with a binder that is less than organized or a planner that has a few too many holes in spaces where assignments should have been written down. I look at each opportunity as a fresh start to make changes. Getting angry or annoyed is just wasted energy; instead, concentrate your efforts on helping your son empower himself to use the strategies to make his (and also your) life simpler and more enriched.

It's Okay to Outsource

I have mentioned this before but it bears repeating: If you are ultimately not the right person to implement some of these strategies with your son given your personal dynamics or for any other reason, it's okay to outsource. Perhaps your parenting partner has a different relationship with your son and could sort through papers with him more effectively, or a close friend or relative would be a better fit to get the habits started and get him to see the win–win nature of becoming more organized. Hiring a tutor or outside counselor could also be the most appropriate solution for your family; indeed, that is how many students find their way to my office. The ultimate

Hiring a tutor or outside counselor could also be the most appropriate solution for your family; indeed, that is how many students find their way to my office.

goal is for him to feel more empowered, so however you get there is the right way to get there.

Any Day Is a Good Day to Start

While it might be easier to start some of these strategies with a new school year or semester (when there is a natural fresh start), I believe that any and every day is an opportunity to make incremental improvements. Start out with a few simple changes and build from there.

Sample Five-Week Strategy

This five-week plan is merely a suggestion; you and your son may immediately implement some changes, whereas others might take your family more time to incorporate. Each family and each student is unique. The reason why this plan works for so many boys and their families is that it is flexible to fit individual needs, so adjust it as needed according to what would work for your son. Five weeks may not be enough time; perhaps you need two weeks (or more) to successfully implement one step's worth of strategies into your lives. Different students pick up on different strategies at different times; just like not everyone learned to walk or read at the same time, each person's ability to grasp some of these concepts is different. Be patient and optimistic—it will happen!

> **TIP:** Each step builds on the one before it, so just because you have moved on to week 2, doesn't mean that your son won't have to organize his binders again and refocus on writing his planner. Each step should take about a week—maybe more, but probably no less. Remember, it's a marathon, not a sprint. Don't rush to move to the next step until you both feel that he is ready. Otherwise, it's too much at once!

Week 1

- Discuss academic and personal goals (Chapter 4).

- Buy necessary supplies (Chapter 5).

- Organize binders and use a written planner (Chapter 5).

- Create a study space and a technology box (Chapter 6).

Week 2

- Set academic and personal goals (Chapter 4).

- Implement two-hour homework blocks (Chapter 7).

- Create a system in which homework is done on the night it's assigned (Chapter 7).

- Fill out a time management chart (Chapter 9).

- Personal health focus: get more sleep (Chapter 9).

Week 3

- Start working toward academic and personal goals (Chapter 4).

- Look at the master schedule and reduce unfulfilling activities (if applicable) (Chapter 9).

- Incorporate strategies for studying for tests and quizzes (Chapter 8).

- Personal health focus: exercise/fitness (Chapter 9).

Week 4

- Work on active reading and related study skills (Chapter 8).

- Personal health focus: diet/nutrition habits (Chapter 9).

Week 5

- Focus on a particular strategy that needs extra attention.

- Revisit academic and personal goals (Chapter 4).

- Personal health focus: doing something fun to reduce stress (Chapter 9).

Good luck!

ACKNOWLEDGMENTS

First and foremost, I would like to thank all the students with whom I have been so fortunate and privileged to work throughout the years. And to their parents, thank you for the wonderful opportunity to work with your children—I truly consider it a gift.

To Steven Rinehart, thanks for all your advice, hard work, thoughts, and background research. Your assistance was truly indispensable, and I am forever grateful.

To Susan Marquess—you introduced me to my first student all the way back in 1995, and you were the one who encouraged me to start working with students again in 2001. Thank you.

To Barbara Stephenson—it was during one of our walks in Portugal that the dream of this book became a reality. Thank you for your support and encouragement.

Many thanks to my wonderful early readers and friends who supported this book (and this writer!) through various stages. Alice Kleeman, whose insight, razor-sharp humor, and editing prowess were priceless. Laura Zimmerman, who always gave me positive support and constructive criticism and whose perspective as a mother was invaluable. Judy Rothenberg, thank you for being my wonderful mentor and having such great feedback for so many chapters of this book. Margaret Miller, your insight on so many aspects of this book was invaluable, and I always look forward to our conversations. Annie, thanks for your friendship and wisdom—my trips to New York City are always that much sweeter with our time together. Alex Jamieson, thanks for giving me the support and encouragement of a true friend. Kara and Mark Edgar, your hospitality was always so amazing in so many ways—thank you.

There were many people who gave so generously of their time to be interviewed for this book and read and commented on related chapters. I hold each of our conversations in such high esteem and am truly thankful: Jane McClure, Nancy Ely, Brewster Ely, Denise Clark Pope, Lindsay Holland, Sallie Sanborn, Jodi Greebel, Kate Burke, Deborah Gee, and several parents who preferred their contributions to be anonymous—you know who you are, and thank you.

To the staff at Green Ivy, who supported me in this crazy endeavor of writing a book, finishing graduate school, and working full-time, all at once—without each of you, it would have been impossible: Lyndsie Schmalz, Becca Velasco, Kat Swanson, Nicole Hinnebusch, and Lisa LoBue. Thank you.

To the wonderful people at Perigee, John Duff and Marian Lizzi, who believed in this book from the very beginning and whose guidance and assistance has made this process much easier than I ever could have imagined—thank you.

To my terrific, sharp, brilliant agent Priscilla Gilman at Janklow and Nesbit, thanks for all your wonderful ways of supporting this book and believing in my mission and my work. Thank you also to Rebecca Gradinger, whose early advice and support put me on the right path.

Finally, to my parents, Amir and Bahereh, who always encourage and believe in my own goals, dreams, and desires, and to my sister, Allia, who keeps it real.

RECOMMENDED READING LIST

Eide, B., and Eide, F. (2006). *The Mislabeled Child: Looking beyond Behavior to Find the True Sources—and Solutions—for Children's Learning Challenges.* New York: Hyperion.

Gurian, Michael. (1997). *The Wonder of Boys.* New York: Putnam.

Kindlon, D., and Thompson, M. (1999). *Raising Cain: Protecting the Emotional Life of Boys.* New York: Ballantine.

Levine, Madeline. (2006). *The Price of Privilege.* New York: HarperCollins.

Pope, Denise Clark. (2001). *Doing School.* New Haven, CT: Yale University Press.

Sax, Leonard. (2007). *Boys Adrift: The Five Factors Driving the Growing Epidemic of Unmotivated Boys and Underachieving Young Men.* New York: Basic Books.

Teyber, Edward. (2001). *Helping Children Cope with Divorce.* San Francisco: Jossey-Bass.

Tyre, Peg. (2008). *The Trouble with Boys.* New York: Crown.

SOURCES

Cline, Foster W., and Jim Fay. (2006). *Parenting with Love and Logic: Teaching Children Responsibility.* Colorado Springs, CO: Pinon Press.

Covey, Nic. (2008). "Flying Fingers; Text-Messaging Overtakes Monthly Phone Calls." Available at http://en-us.nielsen.com/main/insights/consumer_insight/issue_12/flying_fingers.

Foerde, Karin; Barbara J. Knowlton; and Russell A. Poldrack. (2006). Modulation of Competing Memory Systems by Distraction. *Proceedings of the National Academy of Sciences* 103 (31): 11778–11783.

Glaab, L. A.; R. Brown; and D. Daneman. (2005). School Attendance in Children with Type 1 Diabetes. *Diabetic Medicine* 22 (4): 421–426.

GlaxoSmithKline. (2004). "Children and Asthma in America." Available at www.asthmainamerica.com.

Grunbaum, J. A., L. Kann, S. Kinchen, J. Ross, J. Hawkins, R. Lowry, W. A. Harris, T. McManus, D. Chyen, and J. Collins. (2004). Youth Risk Behavior Surveillance—United States, 2003. Atlanta: U.S. Department of Health and Human Services, Centers for Disease Control and Prevention.

Gurian, Michael. (2007). *The Minds of Boys: Saving Our Sons from Falling Behind in School and Life.* San Francisco: Jossey-Bass.

Hannibal, Mary Ellen. (2007). *Good Parenting Through Your Divorce: The Essential*

Guidebook to Helping Your Children Adjust and Thrive Based on the Leading National Program, 2nd ed. Cambridge, MA: Da Capo.

Harris, Henry L., and Doris R. Coy. (2003). Helping Students Cope with Test Anxiety. *ERIC Digest.* Available at www.ericdigests.org/2005-2/anxiety.html.

Harvard Family Research Project. Available at www.hfrp.org/family-involvement/projects.

Hiatt-Michael, Diane B., ed. (2001). *Promising Practices for Family Involvement in Schools.* Charlotte, NC: Information Age.

Juvonen, Jaana, et al. (2004). *Focus on the Wonder Years: Challenges Facing the American Middle School.* Santa Monica, CA: Rand Education.

National Assessment of Educational Progress (NAEP). (2004). Available at http://nces.ed.gov/nationsreportcard.

National Health Interview Survey. (2007). Summary Health Statistics for U.S. Children. Atlanta: Centers for Disease Control and Prevention.

National Sleep Foundation. (2006). "Teens and Sleep." Available at www.sleepfoundation.org/article/sleep-topics/teens-and-sleep.

PBS Frontline. (2002). "Inside the Teenage Brain." Available at www.pbs.org/wgbh/pages/frontline/shows/teenbrain.

Porterfield, Lisa. (2006). "Experts: Despite Their Energy, Kids Still at Risk of Burnout." Available at www.cnn.com/2006/EDUCATION/08/30/overscheduled.kids/index.html.

Post, Steven. (1998). *The Modern Book of Feng Shui: Vitality and Harmony for the Home and Office.* New York: Dell.

Rees, Jonathan. (2003). A Crisis Over Consensus: Standardized Testing in American History and Student Learning. *Radical Pedagogy* 5 (2). Available at http://radicalpedagogy.icaap.org/archives.php.

Shaw, S. R., and P. McCabe. (2008). Hospital to School Transition for Children with Chronic Illness: Meeting the New Challenges of an Evolving Health Care System. *Psychology in the Schools* 45: 74–87.

Teyber, Edward. (2001). *Helping Children Cope with Divorce*, rev. ed. San Francisco: Jossey-Bass.

Thergaonkar, Neerja R. (2007). Brief Report: Relationship Between Test Anxiety and Parenting Style. *Journal of Indian Association for Child and Adolescent Mental Health* 2 (4): 10–12.

Volunteering in America. Available at www.volunteeringinamerica.gov/research_findings/fast_facts.cfm.

LIST OF WORKSHEETS

INDEX